THE WINES
OF THE
COTES DU RHONE

Also by Sheldon Wasserman

THE WINES OF ITALY

THE WINES
OF THE
COTES DU RHONE

SHELDON WASSERMAN

WITH PAULINE WASSERMAN

STEIN AND DAY/*Publishers*/New York

A nos amis, Anne et André

First published in 1977
Copyright © 1977 by Sheldon Wasserman with Pauline Wasserman
All rights reserved
Designed by Ed Kaplin
Printed in the United States of America
Stein and Day/*Publishers*/Scarborough House,
Briarcliff Manor, N.Y. 10510

Library of Congress Cataloging in Publication Data

Wasserman, Sheldon
The Wines of the Côtes du Rhône.

Includes Index.
I. Wasserman, Pauline, joint author. II. Wasserman, Sheldon.
III. Title. 1. Wine and wine making—France—Rhône Valley.
2. Viticulture—France—Rhône Valley.
TP553.W27   641.2'2'09448   76-50066
ISBN 0-8128-2165-3

ACKNOWLEDGMENTS

In writing this book I've gotten help and encouragement from a number of people, and I would like to take this opportunity to thank them.

First, I'd like to express my appreciation to Robert Gourdin, who encouraged me to pursue my interest in things viniferous and who provided many opportunities for me to increase my knowledge of wine.

My thanks to Mel Silverberg and Alfio Moriconi, who encouraged me to write my first article on the wines of the Côtes du Rhône, which eventually led to this book.

And to Mike Smith, who suggested this project to begin with.

To M. Robert LeMercier and M. Jean Pierre Gachlein of the French Consulate, who provided encouragement and much-needed assistance.

To Mme. and M. André Brunel of Châteauneuf-du-Pape, who offered considerable assistance, made my wife and me feel at home at Châteauneuf, translated documents, made helpful suggestions, and even offered driving assistance.

To the Comité Interprofessionnel des Vins des Côtes du Rhône, who gave much assistance, opened many doors, and helped in other ways. To Mlle. Elizabeth Cottarel, who was an able interpreter, and to M. Bernard Ganichaut and M. Roch Lauriol, our helpful guides.

To M. André Canet of Château Grillet, for generously giving of his time and effort.

To M. Max Chapoutier, who provided a lot of useful information and poured some fine wines, and who saw that the American flag was flying at the winery for our arrival.

To M. Chave of Hermitage and M. Robert Jasmin of Côte

5

Rôtie, two of the best vintners I know, who deserve a word of thanks for their generosity in pouring some truly fine wines.

To M. Charles Odoyer of Clos du Palais, Tavel, who provided much valuable information.

I'd also like to thank all of the others who helped the book by providing valuable information and assistance:

M. Jean Jacques Verda and Father James of Château Saint-Roch, Lirac; M. Olivier de Bez of Château d'Aqueria, Tavel; M. Gabriel Roudil, Roudil et Fils, Tavel; M. Hilarion Roux, Domaine Les Pallières, Gigondas; M. Jean Pierre Amadieu, owner and president, Fédération de Gigondas, Gigondas; M. Jean Abeille, Domaine Mont Redon, Châteauneuf-du-Pape; Baron Le Roy Boiseaumarie, Château Fortia, Châteauneuf-du-Pape; M. Maurice Charavin, Domaine du Charavin, Rasteau; M. Maurice Seignour, Mayor of Vacqueyras and wine broker, Vacqueyras; M. Guy Nicolet and M. Remy Nicolet, Chante Perdrix, Châteauneuf-du-Pape; M. Gaston Brunel, Château la Gardine, Châteauneuf-du-Pape; Henri Estevenin, Château Fines Roches Hostellerie, Châteauneuf-du-Pape; the personnel at the Cooperative of Beaumes de Venise; M. Michel Lacrotte, president of the GIE and the Cairanne Cooperative, Cairanne; M. René Riou and M. Jouet, Chapoutier, Tain-l'Hermitage; M. Xavier Frachon and M. Pierre Stephane Chavin, of the Cooperative of Tain; M. Dervieux, president of the Côte Rôtie Syndicate; M. Battier of J. Vidal Fleury; M. André Barge, M. Pierre Barge, and M. Christian Barge, Côte Rôtie; M. Georges Vernay, Condrieu; M. Auguste Clape, Cornas and St.-Péray, and Mme. Marie Laure Meger; and to any others whose names may have been inadvertently left out.

And thanks to Carlo Russo for his splendid introduction to this book.

And to Angelo Charles Castelli, who opened some nice bottles.

To Paul Zimmerman for sharing his 1934 Côte Rôtie "Brune et Blonde" Chapoutier, which, although showing signs of age, was still a marvelous wine with an incredible bouquet and a soft, velvety texture.

I'd like also to thank Patricia Day, my editor, for her many helpful suggestions.

And my wife, Pauline, who thought she didn't want to co-author this book, but who was willing to help, and whose help amounted to more than either of us anticipated.

CONTENTS

INTRODUCTION

Here's a book I'm glad to see written—a book long overdue. And the Wassermans are certainly qualified to do the job. They have written a great deal on wine and related subjects. And their initial enthusiasm for the Rhône wines was increased during their research trip to that area.

There are many wine books on the market. Many are general books and many discuss the same well-known areas. But little has been written on the Côtes du Rhône region. This is an area, in my opinion, too long neglected.

It certainly rates just below Bordeaux and Burgundy in prestige, and in some aspects it's just as important as those two better-known regions. At one time, the Côtes du Rhône wines were considered on a par with the Bordeaux and Burgundies, as the Wassermans point out—when Hermitage, for example, was added to Château Lafite to strengthen it, and it was labeled "Lafite Hermitaged."

After reading the manuscript of *The Wines of the Côtes du Rhône*, I've concluded that the authors' real interest in their subject, and the care and the unquestioned knowledge that went into the writing of this book, have been matched by the depth and accuracy of their research. The result is a book as complete as an encyclopedia, but without its rigid format.

The Wines of the Côtes du Rhône is an easy-flowing account of a wine region deserving to be better known that anyone with an interest in wine, professional or layman, will find rewarding reading.

Carlo Russo
Proprietor, Winés & Spirits, HoHoKus
and Wine World, Wycoff
New Jersey Regional Director of Les Amis du Vin

THE RIVER AND
THE LAND

1. THE RHONE AT ITS SOURCE

Far back in the dim days of prehistory, some twelve thousand years ago, northern and central Europe lay frozen beneath trillions of tons of snow and ice. Only the highest mountain peaks emerged from the depths of this vast glacier in some places as much as one mile thick.

As climatic changes brought warmer temperatures, the glaciers began to melt. In the winter, the snow fell again, but not so much as before. And in the summer, the thaw continued melting all of the winter's snowfall and the frozen surface of the glacier itself. Slowly the landscape thawed, and Europe as we know it today began to emerge.

But remnants of those Ice Age glaciers still remain unmelted high up in the mountain ranges of Austria, France, Germany, and Switzerland. Glaciers covering over 700 square miles are still preserved amid the frozen mountain crests of the Swiss Alps. The most noted of these is the Rhône-gletscher. Over 7,500 feet up in the lofty Furka Pass, this glacier extends for about 8 miles back into the rocky mountain crevasses.

The Furka Pass, generally snowed-in from November to early June, provides a magnificent panorama of the Bernese and Valais Alps. At 7,975 feet, it is the highest pass in the Swiss Alps between Martigny and Chur.

Visitors to the ice cave, cut into the solid ice of the Rhônegletscher, remark at the unusual quality of the bluish light reflected from its walls.

Just below the Rhône glacier, where the Furka Pass road joins the roads from the Grimsel Pass and the Goms Valley, is the little town of Gletsch (altitude 5,776 feet). At one time this spot where the buildings of Gletsch now stand lay buried beneath the lower tip of the Rhône glacier. And records indicate that a few hundred years ago the glacier was more than double its present size. It filled the entire mountain valley. The flow of icy waters from the melting glacier fell in hurtling cascades almost 2,000 feet to the valley floor below. In the warmer climate of the last century the glacier melted steadily. Today the melting continues, but at a slower pace.

VALAIS

It begins with a trickle of melting ice, the ice of the Rhônegletscher. This trickle of icy waters crosses the desolate basin of the Gletschboden and winds its way down to the wide Conches (Goms) Valley. At Brig the milky, steel-colored stream is joined by the waters of the Massa, which flow down from the Aletsch glacier, doubling its volume. (The Aletsch glacier, covering 65 square miles, is the largest in the Alps.) At this point, the Rhône ceases to be a mountain stream and becomes a river flowing across a broad plain between steep rocky mountains.

In the course of its journey from Sierre to Martigny, through the central Valais, the Rhône drains sun-drenched vineyards on the limestone foothills of the Valais mountains. The terraced slopes rise in some places to a height of 4,000 feet. The cultivation of the vine here requires back-breaking labor from the vignerons, who must carry the rain-eroded vineyard soil back up the steep slopes on their backs. It is a situation that is repeated on the Rhône's southerly course past the vineyards of the northern Côtes du Rhône.

The finest vineyards of Switzerland are the vineyards of Valais (the Valley), beginning just below the town of Brig and stretching for 60 miles beside the Rhône river. The best wines of Valais are the white Johannisberg, made from a blend of Sylvaner and Riesling grapes. Fendant, the local name for the Chasselas grape variety, is more common, in acreage and also in quality. Ermitage white is made from the Marsanne grape of Hermitage in the Côtes du Rhône. Some of the other white wines of Valais are Malvoisie, Amigne, and Arvine. Dôle is the region's most highly regarded red. The Visperterminen, a true high-mountain wine, is produced from grapes grown at an altitude of 4,000 feet.

VAUD

Just north of Martigny, where the Rhône is joined by the waters of the Drance, it veers sharply northward, adopting the direction of its tributary.

For the next 20 miles the Rhône tumbles through a narrow rocky gorge carved deeper through the action of the river itself. As it emerges to flow across the valley floor, the vineyards of the Vaud begin to appear along the right bank of the Rhône.

At the southeastern tip of Lake Geneva, the muddy waters of the Rhône river rush into the placid waters of the lake. This tumultuous meeting can be observed from the terraces overlooking Vevey and Montreux.

The dark, roiling waters of the Rhône are not, as they appear to be, quickly swallowed up by the lake. The colder mountain-born current sinks to the bottom of the lake, where it remains at a depth of about 65 feet until the autumn, when the lake water cools and absorbs the river's revitalizing flow. When this 106-mile-long mountain river exits the lake at Geneva, some 45 miles later, it has been transformed into the largest-volume river in France.

Lake Geneva is western Europe's largest lake, covering an area of 143,323 acres and reaching depths of 1,000 feet. It arcs roughly into a crescent shape; at its widest point, between Morges, Switzerland, and Amphion, France, the lake stretches 7½ miles across. Most of the southern shoreline is French. Crépy, a slightly pétillant white wine is produced from the French vineyards cultivated on the hillsides south of the lake. But both tips of the crescent are in Switzerland, as is the northern shore.

Vaud has three wine districts: Lavaux, Chablais, and La Côte. The wines, of Chablais are the most celebrated. Most of the wines of Chablais are white, as are those from the neighboring district of Lavaux. These wines are named for the little hillside villages perched above the lakeside resort towns. Some of the most highly regarded are Aigle, Bex, Cully, Dézaley, Epesses, Ollon, St.-Saphorin, and Yvorne. Salvagnin, from a blend of Pinot noir and Gamay grapes, is perhaps the most-sought-after red wine of the Vaud.

The Route des Vignobles winds its way through the vineyards of the slope—La Côte—between Lausanne and Geneva. The wine villages of Bougy, Féchy, Mont-sur-Rolle, and Vinzel here produce some noted wines.

GENEVA TO LYON

Leaving Geneva and Switzerland behind, the Rhône enters France and crosses a broad undulating valley planted in vines. It flows in a twisted westerly direction through a series of deep gorges in the mountains of the Jura, then veers sharply south near Bellegarde. Here it drains the vineyards of Savoy.

The best wine of Savoy, Şeyssel, takes its name from the

little town of that name. The best Seyssel wines are made
from the Roussette, also known as Altesse, grape variety.
There has been some speculation about this grape. Some
claim it is the Viognier of Condrieu and Château Grillet. But
it could also be the Roussanne, or its improved version,
Roussette, of Hermitage and St.-Péray.

Royale Seyssel and Clos de la Paclette, delicate white
wines from the Roussette grape, rank as two of the better
Seyssel wines. The Molette grape, also grown here, is
considered to produce wines of inferior quality. The red
wines of this area are made from Gamay or Moudeuse grapes.

Savoy is also known for its fine cheeses: Saint-Marcellin,
Comté, Reblochon, and Bleu de Bresse.

Coming out of the Jura mountains, near St.-Genix, the
Rhône makes a sharp right turn to flow northwest of Lagnieu.
There it changes direction once more to flow now south and
west to Lyon.

THE JOURNEY'S END

In Lyon the waters of the Saône join with the Rhône,
which now flows almost due south for some 160 miles.

On its journey southward, the Rhône is joined by
numerous rivers and streams. The Isère flows into the Rhône
just above Cornas; the Ardèche just north of Pont-St.-Esprit;
outside of Orange, the Aygues; the Ouvèze south of
Châteauneuf-du-Pape; below Avignon, the Durance, and the
Gard at Beaucaire.

Just north of Arles the Rhône forks, with the Petit Rhône
flowing west and south, the Grand Rhône south and slightly
east. Both empty into the Mediterranean and thus end the
Rhône's 500-mile journey from a mountain glacier down to
the sea.

Along its journey, the Rhône drains the vineyards of

Valais, in the Vaud on the hills above Lake Geneva, in the mountains of Cevennes and the Jura. Along the steep cliffs of the upper Côtes du Rhône, the Rhône drains the vineyards of Côte Rôtie, Condrieu, Château Grillet, St.-Joseph, Cornas, St.-Péray, Hermitage, and Crozes-Hermitage; on the broad plain of the lower Côtes du Rhône, the vineyards of the Côtes du Rhône Villages, Rasteau, Beaumes de Venise, Gigondas, Châteauneuf-du-Pape, Lirac, and Tavel.

2. THE VINE IN THE COTES DU RHONE

The Rhône river has been a highway between the Mediterranean and northern Europe since at least the time of the Greeks, some 2,500 years ago. Some accounts credit the Greek founders of Massilia (Marseille) with establishing this trade route. It is a supposition that seems reasonable, but it has not been proved.

One thing does seem certain, though, and that is that the Phocaean Greeks from Ionia introduced the Gauls to wine. When they settled Massilia in 600 B.C., they planted the vines they had brought with them on the hills around the town. According to Strabo, these vineyards flourished.

They traded wine and ceramics to the Celtic tribes for iron, amber, and furs. In this trade the beer-drinking tribes were civilized, you might say, through their introduction to among other things the pleasures of the grape.

Greek amphorae from the sixth century B.C. have been found in the upper Saône valley as well as in the Jura.

This wine from Massilia was smoked to give it staying power. Martial referred to it in a derogatory manner as *"Cocta fumis musta Massilitanis"*—Massiliot wine cooked in smoke. The Italians considered this wine vile stuff. But the Celtic and Germanic tribes who traded for it found it quite acceptable. They didn't know any better, and it was apparently an improvement over the beer they were drinking. We have no descriptions of what their beer was like.

The Massilians weren't the only ones who resorted to unusual methods to try to improve their wine. The wine-makers of Narbonne were reputedly doctoring their wines with herbs and colorants as well as smoke, making them, in a sense, a sort of vermouth.

In 538 BC, after the Cypriot conquest of Asia Minor, more Ionian Greeks settled in Gaul, founding the cities of Monöikos (Monaco), Nikai (Nice), and Antipoles (Antibes.)

The town of Ampuis was, according to some scholars, founded about this time by the Phocaean Greeks who had settled Massilia some years earlier. Cornas also was supposed to have been settled by these same Greeks at about this time. These Greek settlers are reputed to have planted the first vines in these parts.

Martial, Ovid, and Pliny the Younger all mention a wine believed to have been the wine of Cornas. The Allobroges, a Gallic tribe whose domain extended east to Geneva and west across the Rhône into the land of Arvernii, grew vines in, or in the vicinity of, the Isère Valley. The Isère river empties into the Rhône near Cornas.

Columella, Martial, and Plutarch refer to Viennois en Allobrogie and Vinum Picatum, wines that came from the area around Vienne. Some believe that these wines, or at least one of them, came from the steep hillside vineyards above, below, and behind the village of Ampuis.

These wines had a slight taste of pitch, which supposedly was a characteristic of the grape varieties used. Vinum Picatum, as the name implies, came from the Picata grape; Allobrogica was the grape of Viennois en Allobrogie. The Allobrogica variety was supposed to be able to withstand cold spells and even frost, which gave it an advantage in this more northerly clime.

Vinum Picatum and Viennois en Allobrogie were popular wines with the Romans in the early years of the Christian era.

It would seem they liked the piney taste of pitch. They sometimes added resin to their wine, as the Greeks do today. Pliny didn't favor these wines, but he does say that they had a certain renown in about AD 60, and had been made for some time before.

Vinum Passum, a wine from dried grapes or raisins, was also produced in the Côtes du Rhône during this period.

In the second century BC the Gauls attacked Massilia. They had cast an envious eye on the rich markets, luxurious houses, and well-ordered countryside. Greece being a thousand miles away, the Massilians appealed to Rome to come to their aid in 125 BC.

The Romans unhesitatingly came to the rescue. And though Massilia remained a free city, the rest of the region came under Roman rule then, and remained so for about eight centuries.

In 122 BC the Romans founded Aquae Sextiae (Aix-en-Provence) and shortly afterwards, the Roman towns of Nîmes, Avignon, Arles, Vaison-la-Romaine, Valence, Orange, and Lyon. Roman legions occupied Vienne, the capital of the Allobroges, in 121 BC.

They crisscrossed the countryside with roads and aqueducts. Today you can see many majestic ruins from that era. Roman triumphal arches, arenas, amphitheaters, aqueducts, baths, and the remains of whole Roman cities are scattered throughout this once-Roman province, Provence, and northward to Lyon.

Condrieu, according to ancient writings, was founded in 58 BC by a Helvetian tribe from the Swiss lowlands. This tribe was sent, or probably driven, there by Julius Caesar. Some of the terraces on the nearby hillsides reputedly date from this Roman period. The Latin poet Martial describes the wine of Condrieu.

Condrieu is made from the Viognier grape. This grape

variety is reported to have been introduced here from Dalmatia by the Roman Emperor Probus (276-282). Probus also gets credit for rescinding the decree of Domitian, which ordered at least half of the vines in the provinces torn out, and prohibited the extension of vineyards in Italy.

Some writers believe this edict was designed to protect Italian wines from competition that was becoming quite fierce. Suetonius in his biography *The Twelve Caesars* says that in about AD 90 Domitian became concerned that the grains were being neglected when a bumper crop from the vineyards followed on the heels of a poor grain harvest, but that the edict wasn't enforced although it remained in effect for nearly two centuries.

Probus not only repealed the edict, but ordered the legions to work in the vineyards of Gaul.

The Syrah grape is believed to have been brought here from either Syracuse, from which it derived its name, by Greeks, or from Persia, where it was known as Shiraz, by returning crusaders. Helvenacia minor, another variety known to have been grown in this area at about the same time, was, according to the noted ampelographers Viala and Vermorel, either the Pinot noir or an earlier version of it.

Local belief holds that St.-Péray was the site of the Vinum Picatum vineyards noted by Pliny and Plutarch.

Besides the usual Roman artifacts—ceramics, coins, and the like—a store of about forty wine amphorae were found near Tain-l'Hermitage. Columella, Martial, Pliny, and Plutarch mention the wine from this general area, and this wine could well have been the forerunner of today's Hermitage.

Speculation has it that the Gauls made wine near Rasteau even before the coming of the Romans. There is little, if any, evidence to support the view that either the Gauls or the Romans did actually make wine here, but the Roman town of Vaison-la-Romaine is nearby.

Gallo-Roman ruins at Beaumes de Venise as well as a reference to the Muscat of Balme (Beaume) by Pliny lend credence to the view that the Romans made wine here. Local growers credit the Greek founders of Massilia with first planting the Muscat vine here, about 2,500 years ago.

The village of Tavel, known then as Tavellis, dates from the Roman period. Roman ruins and artifacts have been found in this area. But no wine is known to have been made here prior to the ninth century, when the rosé of Tavel was written about.

Roman ruins have been found also at Roquemaure. It is believed that the Romans produced wines in this vicinity, if not at Roquemaure, then possibly at Lirac.

Roman legions camped close by Gigondas (Jiguit Undas, in Latin) and were supposed to have produced wine here. Pliny mentions this wine.

Roman artifacts were found also at Châteauneuf-du-Pape, but wine was probably not made there until a century or so before the popes settled in at Avignon.

The wine town of Vacqueyras also has its Roman artifacts.

Julius Caesar himself camped nearby the village of Laudun. And traces of a vineyard from that time have been found, making this the oldest wine-producing town (so far as we know) of the area.

It would seem that most of the major vineyard areas of the Côtes du Rhône were planted before the end of the Roman era by either the Greeks or the Romans. Thus the vineyards of the Côtes du Rhône and Provence are the oldest wine-growing areas in France.

As the Roman legions moved north, they cultivated the grape on the steep banks of the northern Côtes du Rhône. From Greece and Rome, the grape traveled up the Rhône to Burgundy, the Moselle, and the Rhine.

The Romans had brought the vine to this area, and along with it their own civilized culture. With their downfall, other invaders stormed in to destroy that civilization. In the fifth century AD, the Franks, a Germanic tribe, swept down from the north and ran roughshod through the area. A long period of intermittent invasion and warfare ensued. The scimitar-wielding armies of the Moors invaded from the south. Religious scruples prevented the Moors from drinking alcoholic beverages, but they had no scruples about enforcing their religious views on others. These were dark days indeed for the people of the Côtes du Rhône.

When the Roman Empire collapsed, Provence was among the first provinces to fall, and it was one of the first to emerge from the Dark Ages.

Burgundians settled in the Rhône Valley. In time, control of this area passed from the Burgundians to the church. The heyday of Provençal culture, with its poets and troubadours singing the praises of courtly love, was between the tenth and fourteenth centuries.

Monks planted vineyards at St.-Péray and Cornas in the tenth century. Knights Templar cultivated the vine at Châteauneuf-du-Pape a few centuries later. By the fourteenth century, all the major wine districts of the Côtes du Rhône were established and known.

The fourteenth century brought the popes to Avignon during the "Babylonian captivity." They exerted considerable influence on the viticulture of the region under their control. They are credited with the introduction of white wine in Châteauneuf-du-Pape. Believing that a less alcoholic wine would be more suitable for the mass, the early morning mass especially, the pope requested that a white wine be made for the *vin de messe*.

The popes also extended the vineyards in the Comtat

Venaissin, which was papal territory. And monks were sometimes sent to the villages to help with the harvest.

It was the power of the church, too, that almost brought the making of the Muscat of Beaumes de Venise to an end. This onetime favorite of the popes was severely limited by strict regulations on its making and its drinking by a high church official outraged at the sometimes drastic results of overconsumption. The story has a happy ending, though—these immoderate regulations were rescinded in the end, and the Muscat wine revived.

In the second half of the last century a plague hit the vineyards of the Côtes du Rhône, of France, of Europe, and almost the whole world. This was *Phylloxera vastatrix*, and it threatened to wipe out the *Vitis vinifera* and bring to an end the enjoyment of fine wine.

Phylloxera was first discovered in a greenhouse in Hammersmith, England, in 1863. At about this same time the first damage from phylloxera in the vineyards of France was noted at Pujualt in the Gard, north of Arles. By 1867 the stricken areas had reached alarming proportions, the pest having attacked vineyards at Corntat, Crau, in parts of the Alps, and around Tarascon. Vineyards in the departments of Gard and Vaucluse in the Côtes du Rhône had also been hit.

The cause of the damage was not identified until 1868, the same year the effects of the phylloxera plague were first noted at Roquemaure in the Côtes du Rhône. It was discovered that a particularly virulent plant louse was the cause of the problem.

This root louse was named *Phylloxera vastatrix*, "leaf-witherer, the devastator." The leaves of the vine were where the first fatal signs of its attack were noticed.

Usually the infestation began with a vine or two in the midst of the vineyard. These vines sickened, and their leaves yellowed. A reddening of the leaf edges followed. Finally the leaves dried up and fell off. In the next year the symptoms were worse, and the damage spread to the neighboring vines. By the third year, the vines were dead.

Many vignerons, in despair at the phylloxera's destruction and seeming imperviousness to any measures taken against it, left the vineyards to find work in the cities. Others stayed and planted crops which could grow in the poor soil and dry climate where the vine had thrived—before this disaster struck. Vineyards were ripped up and abandoned. The worst period of the scourge's destruction was in the late 1880s.

After a long investigation it was discovered that phylloxera had come from the United States. This tiny parasite lives on the roots of some native American grape varieties, which are immune to it.

American vines had been imported into Europe from 1629 onward. Why did damage from phylloxera not occur until as late as 1863?

The answer lies in the slow ships—by the time the vines arrived in Europe, the louse was dead. But by the early 1860s, steamships were speeding across the oceans, and railroads reduced inland travel time. The time was short enough for phylloxera to survive the journey, and begin its destruction of the vineyards of the world.

It was an unknown enemy, but eventually a defense was found. And like the louse itself, it also came from America— resistant American rootstock. Now virtually all European vines are grafted onto American roots. And the world can once again enjoy the fine wines of the Côtes du Rhône.

3. THE WINES OF THE COTES DU RHONE

Sitting comfortably at your window seat on the rapid train between Lyon and Avignon, the "Mistral," you surge past the vineyards of the Côtes du Rhône as fast as the Mistral itself, that fierce wind that whips down through the Valley of the Rhône bending the trees into a permanent tilt.

The vineyards of the Côtes du Rhône, covering some 100,000 acres (40,000 hectares), are planted on both sides of the Rhône river between the Massif Central and the Alps. The vineyards extend for 125 miles from Vienne to Avignon—with the interruption of a 40-mile vineless gap—and into six departments: the eastern parts of the Rhône, Loire, Ardèche, and Gard on the west bank of the Rhône and the western sections of Drôme and Vaucluse on the east bank.

Most of the wines of the Rhône department, interestingly enough, are produced in the Beaujolais region, north of Lyon and not part of the Côtes du Rhône. But the two northernmost Côtes du Rhône appellations are in that department—Côte Rôtie and Condrieu, which extends into the department of Loire.

Appellation Contrôlée (AC) means that the wine in question is officially recognized by the French government. The government defines the regulations governing the viticulture and viniculture of every AC wine. The regulations are enforced by the Institut National des Appellations d'Origine des Vins et Eaux-de-Vie (INAO). AC is an official recognition of origin and authenticity, not a guarantee of quality.

The only sparkling wine of the Côtes du Rhône, the *mousseux* of St.-Péray, is produced in Ardèche. The Drôme department spans the northern and southern regions of the Côtes du Rhône.

Vaucluse has, by far, the heaviest concentration of vineyards in the Côtes du Rhône. Both in acreage and in output of AC Côtes du Rhône wines, Vaucluse is ahead of all the other five departments combined. Gard, in terms of total vinicultural output, is the third-largest wine-producing department of France.

But most of the wine of Gard is from the Midi. The Gard department runs from the lower Côtes du Rhône well into the Midi.

Appellations by Department	Extent of Vineyards		Appellation
	ACRES	HECTARES	
Rhône	200	80	Côte Rôtie
			Condrieu
Loire	50	20	Condrieu
			Château Grillet
Ardèche	1,080	435	St.-Joseph
			Cornas
			St.-Péray
Drôme	24,000	9,625	Hermitage
			Crozes-Hermitage
			Côtes du Rhône Villages
			Rochegude
			Rousset
			St.-Maurice

Appellations by Department	Extent of Vineyards		Appellation
	ACRES	HECTARES	
			St.-Pantaléon
			Vinsobres
Vaucluse	55,000	22,000	Rasteau
			Beaumes de Venise
			Gigondas
			Châteauneuf-du-Pape
			Côtes du Rhône Villages
			Cairanne
			Gigondas
			Rasteau
			Roaix
			Séguret
			Vacqueyras
			Valréas
			Visan
Gard	20,000	8,000	Tavel
			Lirac
			Côtes du Rhône Villages
			Chusclan
			Laudun

Average total production of all the Côtes du Rhône wines covered under AC from 1973 through 1975 was approximately 40 million gallons, or 1.5 million hectoliters, a year.

The regional AC Côtes du Rhône covers red, white, and rosé wines. The wines of the Côtes du Rhône, both red and white, are fuller and fruitier than those of its northern neighbor, Burgundy. Because of their higher alcohol content, they have more body than the "big, fat Burgundies."

Vintage	White Wine		Red and Rosé Wine	
	GALLONS	HECTOLITERS	GALLONS	HECTOLITERS
1973	454,583	17,180	45,675,861	1,726,223
1974	436,484	16,496	39,605,196	1,496,795
1975	357,025	13,493	31,583,661	1,193,638
Average	416,031	15,723	38,954,906	1,472,219

Overall, the red wines of the Côtes du Rhône are medium dark to dark red wines, big-bodied, full-flavored, and fruity. Most mature within a few years of the vintage and can be drunk young, though they usually improve with some age. They should generally be given a minimum of one to three years in bottle, and be drunk before their fifth or sixth year.

The whites are golden in color. They also require one to two years in bottle to soften and develop, and are among the longest-lived dry white wines of the world.

The rosés vary in color from medium pink to coral. They have, when young, a fresh, fruity aroma and a dry, pleasing taste. As a general rule, they are best consumed before their third year.

Besides red, white, and rosé, certain local ACs allow sparkling and fortified wines.

Appellations by Type	Red	White	Rosé
Côtes du Rhône	x	x	x
Côtes du Rhône Villages	x	x	x
Côte Rôtie	x		
Condrieu		x	
Château Grillet		x	
St.-Joseph	x	x	
Cornas	x		

Appellations by Type	Red	White	Rosé
St.-Péray		x	
Hermitage	x	x	
Crozes-Hermitage	x	x	
Gigondas	x		x
Châteauneuf-du-Pape	x	x	
Tavel			x
Lirac	x	x	x

OTHERS

St.-Péray—Mousseux (sparkling)

Rasteau—Vin Doux Naturel
      Vin de Liqueur

Beaumes de Venise—Vin Doux Naturel

Hermitage—Vin de Paille

THE LAND

The Côtes du Rhône, viticulturally, is actually two regions in one. The northern and southern sections differ not only in soil, climate, and terrain, but also in cultivation and styles of vinification.

The northern region, from Vienne to Valence, includes the vineyards of Côte Rôtie, Condrieu, Château Grillet, St.-Joseph, Cornas, St-Péray, Hermitage, and Crozes-Hermitage. These wines are less robust, less alcoholic, more delicate, slower-maturing, and longer-lived than those of the southern region.

In the north the Rhône Valley is narrow. The vines are planted on steeply terraced granite cliffs with outcroppings of chalk, silicate, and limestone, and a high proportion of pebbles.

Between the northern and southern regions, from just below Valence to near Pierrelatte, where the valley widens, is a stretch of barren, desolate land—well, not barren and desolate exactly, there are cereals, fruit, and other crops, but there are no vines.

In the southern section are the vineyards of the Côtes du Rhône Villages, Rasteau, Beaumes de Venise, Gigondas, Châteauneuf-du-Pape, Lirac, and Tavel. These wines are high in alcohol, full-bodied, fruitier, and faster-maturing than those from the northern Côtes du Rhône.

The soil here is clay and limestone with admixtures of iron oxide and, in some areas, sand. Some of the vineyards, notably those of Châteauneuf-du-Pape are covered with stones—they call them "pebbles" there but in some cases to say "boulders" might give you a better picture—well, large rocks anyway. The terrain here ranges from flat to undulating.

The northern Côtes du Rhône has a continental climate; the southern section, a Mediterranean one.

Both regions experience the Mistral, a strong, cold, dry wind that sweeps down from the north through the entire length of the Côtes du Rhône. Once the Mistral begins it lasts for at least three to four days before it subsides. It sometimes rages for a few weeks at a time—and at that point perhaps the windblown populace begins to rage also. Cypress trees and lombardy poplars are planted as windbreaks and in some places fences of reeds have been put up for protection for the vines.

The weather in the north is more varied. It rains more often—which is not to say that it rains often; it doesn't, but it is not as dry as the south.

The sun is less intense here and the grapes don't ripen as

easily as in the southern section. The alcoholic minimum in the north is lower, varying from 10% to 11%; as opposed to the 11% to 12.5% of the south. Some villages in the north are allowed to achieve their alcoholic minimum with the aid of chaptalization. But this is never allowed in the southern Côtes du Rhône.

Chaptalization is the addition of sugar to the grape juice (must) prior to fermentation to increase the alcoholic level of the resultant wine. It is done when the grapes lack sufficient sugar to produce an acceptable wine.

The southern Côtes du Rhône is a region of abundant sunshine and very little rain. (November is a little damp.) As Waverley Root says, "The first fact of life in Provence is the sun. . . . The sun has made Provence a country of painters, some native, some attracted to it by the luminosity of its colors." This area, which is partly in Provence, is provençal in its climate, its cuisine, and in the sunny outlook of its people.

In the background is the song of the *cigale*, a cricketlike insect that chirps a rhythmic tune. The air here is filled with the scent of wild herbs—thyme, lavender, rosemary, and laurel. And the aroma of some of the wines reflects this spiciness.

THE VARIETIES

Another difference between the northern and southern areas is the number of grape varieties used in the wines. The wines from the north (other than the regional Côtes du Rhônes) cannot combine more than three of the only four allowable varieties; the southern wines can be made from as many as twenty different grapes.

With the exception of the *vins doux naturels* of Rasteau

and Beaumes de Venise, all the ACs in the southern section are allowed to use at least nine different grape varieties. Gigondas and Côtes du Rhône Villages may use most of the varieties allowed for the regional Côtes du Rhône AC; Châteauneuf-du-Pape is allowed thirteen varieties, Lirac eleven, and Tavel nine.

This diversity of grapes means that the wines of the southern Côtes du Rhône will be produced in a wider range of types, even within a single AC.

This is varied further by the fact that in some parts of the south different types of vinification are also used—the traditional method and the semi-carbonic maceration method (discussed in Chapter 17, Châteauneuf-du-Pape); and sometimes the wine is a blend of both.

In the north it is only the traditional method that ferments the wine for long periods on the skins and with the stems, then keeps it in wood casks for aging.

What kind of wood? Well, the vintners in the Côtes du Rhône seem very casual about this—by California standards, at least. When asked they will usually answer, "*Chêne*" (oak), or sometimes also chestnut. But what kind of oak? A shrug—Russian, Slavonic, some French. One or two even had American oak. Not the French oak of Limousin, Nevers, etc., the pride of the California cellar? Well, yes, of course, French oak, too. But the native oak wasn't considered as fine as the imported oak from the forests of eastern Europe.

The wines of the regional AC Côtes du Rhône can be made with any or all of twenty-four different grape varieties. The thirteen most common, or principal, varieties are Bourboulenc, Carignane or Carignan, Cinsault or Cinsaut, Clairette, Grenache, Marsanne, Mourvèdre, Picardin, Picpoul or Piquepoul, Roussanne or the improved version

Roussette, Syrah, Terret noir, and Viognier. Eleven less common, or secondary varieties are also allowed: Calitor, Camarèse, Counoise, Gamay noir à jus blanc, Maccabéo or Maccabeau, Mauzac, Muscardin, Pascal blanc, Pinot fin de Bourgogne, Ugni blanc, and Vaccarèse.

The secondary varieties in total may not exceed 30%. Among the principal varieties, Carignan in its three types— Carignan noir, blanc, and gris—may not exceed 30%. This variety is looked down upon today and is gradually being replaced. The Grenache noir, blanc, and gris, too, are slowly being replaced by varieties considered superior. Syrah, widely planted in the north, is one of the varieties replacing Carignane and Grenache in the southern Côtes du Rhône.

The varieties used in the Côtes du Rhône are multi-national. Bourboulenc, Cinsault, and Clairette, among others, are French varieties; Mourvèdre, Grenache, and Carignane are Spanish imports. (Carignane was introduced into France in the twelfth century from Carineru, a region in Aragon.) From Italy, there is the Trebbiano, or Ugni blanc as it is known here. (In Cognac this variety is known as St.-Emilion. Another brandy variety, Picpoul, known in Armagnac as Folle Blanche, also grows here.)

With this profusion of allowable varieties, why would anyone plant the so-called French-American hybrids? These hybrid varieties were developed in the last century from crosses between the French vinifera and American native varieties when the vinifera vineyards were devastated by phylloxera.

A better solution was found in grafting vinifera vines onto American rootstock, which does not affect the quality of the wine, although some who have tasted pre-phylloxera wines maintain their reservations—how could anything match those grand old wines? But newer methods of cultivation and winemaking have probably made a much more significant change in the wines than rootstock ever did.

To prevent the proliferation of these high-yielding, low-quality hybrids, French AC laws forbid their use. All of the wine from any vineyard growing hybrids is automatically declassified to *vin ordinaire*—none of the wine from that vineyard can be labeled as an AC wine. In Châteauneuf-du-Pape if a winery even has hybrid wine in the cellar, all of its wine is declassified.

The maximum yield allowed for regional Côtes du Rhône wines is 535 gallons/acre (50 hectoliters/hectare). Over the centuries it has been found that the best grapes are produced on vines that have been well pruned. These vines, naturally, produce fewer bunches, but they have fruitier grapes. The strength of the vine is concentrated in the few bunches. When the vines are overcropped—pruned to produce more quantity—quality suffers.

Minimum alcoholic content is 11%, which must be achieved naturally. Under no circumstances is chaptalization permitted. Some local ACs, such as Côte Rôtie and Hermitage in the north, allow chaptalization and set a lower alcoholic minimum (10%). If these wines do not meet their AC standards and are declassified, they cannot use the regional Côtes du Rhône AC unless the wines have achieved 11% alcohol naturally; otherwise they must be sold simply as *vin ordinaire*.

BRANDY AND MARC

AC regulations also apply to brandy and marc made in the Côtes du Rhône. To qualify for this AC, the wine to be distilled must be made only from those grape varieties allowed for AC Côtes du Rhône.

The wine can be made into brandy, or the skins, pips, and stalks which remain after pressing distilled into marc.

The type of still, its capacity, and the method of heating is regulated by the AC laws—very little is left to an innovative imagination. Maximum alcoholic level after distillation is 142°. Maximum alcohol at the time of sale is 80°. Brandy or marc, to qualify for *appellation réglementée*, must be approved by a tasting committee appointed by INAO.

Chapoutier, one of the Côtes du Rhône's most notable *négociants*, produces a Marc Vieux and a Fine Eau de Vie des Côtes du Rhône. These brandies are aged in small oak casks for fifteen years, topped up as needed with older brandies.

(*Négociant* may be loosely translated as a producer-shipper. A *négociant* buys grapes and/or wine, makes and/or finishes the wine, matures it, bottles it, and then sells it. The producer-shippers in the Côtes du Rhône often own vineyards as well.)

Vidal Fleury is another producer-shipper making brandy and marc from Côtes du Rhône wines. Some of the other producers and shippers do the same.

The brandy of Châteauneuf-du-Pape, like the wine of that area, is quite spicy.

THE PRODUCERS

As there are many small holders in the southern Côtes du Rhône, the viniculture of that area is characterized by large growers' cooperatives. Practically every major wine town has one. The northern Côtes du Rhône, on the other hand, has only one true cooperative, that of Tain-l'Hermitage. It is not that the growers in the north own vast tracts of land—they don't. But relatively speaking, their holdings are larger, and their wines fetch higher prices. This makes it more feasible for the grower to produce his own wine even when he owns a small plot—in Côte Rôtie, for example, some grower-producers own a vineyard of only 2.5 acres (1 hectare).

In the southern Côtes du Rhône, there are numerous large cooperatives which make the wine, age the wine in cooperage, bottle it, and label and sell it under the name of the co-op. The owners of the cooperative are the member growers who supply the grapes from their vineyards. Basically, these growers have pooled their resources to be able to buy efficient modern equipment—pressers, de-stemmers (*égrappoirs*), fermenters, bottling equipment, and better cooperage and cellaring.

Châteauneuf-du-Pape is the only local appellation in the southern Côtes du Rhône that doesn't have a true cooperative. They do have two bottling-storage co-ops, the most famous being the Reflets de Châteauneuf-du-Pape, a union of some half-dozen producers each making his own wine but bottling it and storing the bottles at the Cave Reflets. A few years ago a second cooperative bottling and storage cellar was organized in Châteauneuf.

In the north, ten producers in St.-Péray have a cooperative cellar for making their sparkling (*mousseux*) wine. Each producer makes his own still St.-Péray wine, then brings it to the co-op cellar where it is made into *mousseux* by the Champagne method (see Chapter 9).

Shippers in both sections of the Côtes du Rhône, as in Burgundy, Alsace, the Loire, and other regions, buy grapes and wine. They make or finish the wine and mature it, then bottle, label, and sell it under their name. Some of the shippers own vineyards as well. Chapoutier, Fleury, Delas, Jaboulet, and Jaboulet-Vercherre are among the bigger and better ones.

Besides the cooperatives and the shippers there are many independent producers who grow their own grapes, make their own wine, mature it, bottle it, label it, and market it under their own name.

A recent development in the Côtes du Rhône was the formation in 1975, of the Groupement d'Intérêt Economique (GIE) Présence des Côtes du Rhône. The GIE, an association of 5,000 growers, producers, and cooperatives, was formed to market Côtes du Rhône wines. It is, in effect, similar to a shipper except that it doesn't make or age the wine. It only markets it.

The GIE represents (potentially) over half of the production of the entire Côtes du Rhône. The GIE sells its wines—which represent the whole range of Côtes du Rhône wines—in the United States under the Rhônecôte label.

The members of the GIE include some of the finest producers of the Côtes du Rhône. One unfortunate thing is that these producers' names do not appear on the labels of the Rhônecôte wines. But these wines are not blends of the wines of multiple producers; they are individually produced and bottled.

A partial list of some of the more important Rhônecôte grower-producers in the northern Côtes du Rhône:

Côte Rôtie—Barges, Bonnefond, Champet, Dervieux, Guerin, Jasmin; Condrieu—Vernay; Château Grillet—Canet; St.-Joseph—Gripa, Co-op of Tain; Cornas—Clape; St.-Péray—Clape; Hermitage—Chave, Grippat, Sorrel, Domaine de l'Hermite, Crozes-Hermitage—Co-op of Tain.

The member "cooperatives" in the southern Côtes du Rhône, not all true cooperatives:

Cave Coopérative "Les Coteaux du Rhône," Sérignan; Union des Vignerons de l'Enclave des Papes, Valréas; Cave Coopérative "La Vigneronne," Villedieu; Cave Coopérative des Coteaux de Cairanne; Les Vignerons de Roaix-Séguret; Les Vignerons de Gigondas; Cave Coopérative de St.-Laurent des Arbres; Cave Coopérative des Vignerons de Tavel; Cave Coopérative "Les Vignerons de Chusclan"; Cave Coopérative des Vignerons de Roquemaure; Cave Coopérative de St.-Hilaire d'Ozilhan; Les Vins Fins de Laudun et Côtes du Rhône; Les Vignerons de Castellas à Rochefort du Gard; Cave Coopérative des Coteaux du Grès, Orange; Le Cellier des Princes, Courthézon; Coopérative des Producteurs de Châteauneuf-du-Pape.

This last, Coopérative des Producteurs de Châteauneuf-du-Pape, makes a special cuvée for Rhônecôte of twenty different wines from twenty different growers.

There are twenty-one members of this cooperative, all noted producers of Châteauneuf-du-Pape, including André Brunel, president of the Coopérative, Nicolet Frères, M. Jamet (Courthézon), Joseph Sabon, and Paul Jean.

In 1975 they made their first cuvée, of 5,292 gallons (200 hectoliters), a blend of 265 gallons (10 hectoliters) of 1973 wines from twenty different growers.

For their second cuvée, in 1976, they selected twenty wines from twenty-eight 1974s submitted. Some producers had to present three different wines to have one selected—the standards of the cooperative are high. The wines are blended together in December and bottled in May.

The cooperative plans, at least for the foreseeable future, to continue to produce its cuvée from a blend of twenty different two-year-old wines. This Châteauneuf-du-Pape wine will be sold in the United States under the Rhônecôte label.

The Union des Vignerons de l'Enclave des Papes in Valréas is a union of four cooperatives.

Under the name of the vineyard, the producer, the co-op, the shipper, or Rhônecôte, the wines of the Côtes du Rhône should become better known. The Côtes du Rhône offers the wine drinker a wide range of choices: sparkling and still wines, fortified dessert and aperitif wines, big, robust reds, full-flavored whites, and dry, fruity rosés, even brandy and marc. And some of these are among the best the wine world has to offer.

THE NORTHERN
COTES DU RHONE

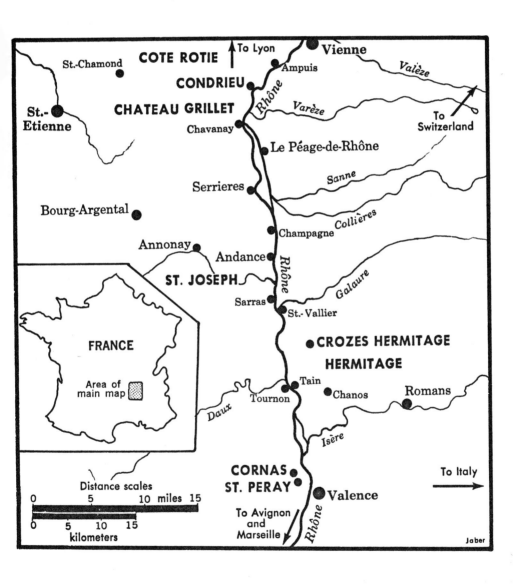

4. COTE ROTIE

Of all the great wines of the world, the wines of Côte Rôtie have maintained their reputation for the longest period. The origins of this wine reputedly date back to 500 BC, to the time of the Greek Phocaeans of Aeolius, founders of Marseilles, Nice, and Antibes.

The Syrah grape, widely grown in the northern Côtes du Rhône, is thought to have been brought to France from Syracuse by the Greeks who founded the village of Ampuis, which sits below the slopes of Côte Rôtie. The historian Cochard and Professor Claudius Roux credit the Phocaean Greeks from Aeolius with settling Ampuis around 500 BC.

The wines of Côte Rôtie, which might, then, be the most ancient vineyard of the Côtes du Rhône, were also known and appreciated by the Romans. They enjoyed the Vinum Picatum, believed to be from the vineyards around Ampuis. This wine, according to the descriptions of Pliny, Plutarch and others, had a slight taste of pitch. This was not from being resinated, though; the slightly piney flavor came from the grape variety, Picata. The poet and agriculturist Columella, Martial, and Plutarch sang its praises. Pliny seems to have had some reservations—he might have got an off bottle, or goatskin, as that was how the wine was "bottled."

With the variations among bottles that we still get sometimes, imagine what it was like in those days. (Uniformity? Didn't that have something to do with the way the Roman legions were outfitted? It surely couldn't have referred to goatskins of wine.) And then again, maybe this wine just wasn't to Pliny's taste.

Also highly regarded during the Roman era was the wine known as Viennois en Allobrogie. It too had, according to the ancient writers, a taste of pitch, a characteristic of the grape variety the wine was made from, Allobrogica. If grapes sometimes had more than one name then, and they probably did (they often do now), these two with the hint of pine could well have been the same variety. This grape was named for the Allobroges tribe whose capital was at Vienne.

The town of Vienne, north of the vineyards, was occupied by Roman legions as early as 121 BC. Some impressive Roman ruins, including the beautiful and well-preserved temple of Augustus and Livia, still stand as monuments to Vienne's ancient past.

Some 4 miles downstream from Vienne, around the bend of the Rhône, precipitous, stony hills loom into view terraced with old stone walls and covered with vines that seem to cling to the hillsides. These are the vineyards of Côte Rôtie, the "roasted slope." It is a fitting description; this hillside and its vines facing south and east are exposed to the heat of the bright sun's rays the whole day long. Protected by the high mountains to the west, Côte Rôtie is the northernmost appellation of the Côtes du Rhône.

The hills, with some of the steepest vineyards of the Côtes du Rhône, have been terraced to make the cultivation of the vine possible here. Some of the terraces are so tiny that there's room for only five or six vines. The retaining walls, called "cheys" or "murgeys" here, were built by dry construction, without benefit of cement, and in some places incorporate the living rock of the hillside in their construction.

The terracing of the hills helps to retain the valuable

vineyard soil. Well, valuable for the vine—the soil is stony and poor. But perhaps there is something to the theory that wine, like people, develops character in the struggle against adversity, and the best wines come from the seemingly least favored vineyards. This wine is the best red of the entire Côtes du Rhône, and one of the greatest of France.

Even with the terracing, some of the soil is washed down the hill by the rains and must be laboriously carried back up on a man's back. This and the other hand labor necessary to maintain these vineyards is back-breaking work, literally.

The old ways persist, however, because mechanization is made impossible by the steepness of the slope, ranging from 656 to 919 feet (200-280 meters) in height, and averaging 100 yards from top to bottom at a gradient of 30 to 35 degrees.

These vineyards are among the most expensive to maintain and many of the terraces have been abandoned.

Workers leave the vineyards for the factories where the work is easier, less demanding, and the pay higher. However, because of the higher prices the wines of Côte Rôtie have brought in recent years, producers have been able to offer higher wages. Consequently, about five years ago, some of the workers began to return.

American investment capital has helped to keep some of the vineyards here in production. M. Chapoutier, one of the area's most important producer-shippers, says that the growers continue to produce a Côte Rôtie wine to keep the AC, but that it doesn't even pay for itself. It has become an old-fashioned luxury, which I, for one, am happy to still have the chance to indulge in.

The *Appellation Contrôlée* laws set the maximum yield at 375 gallons/acre (35 hectoliters/hectare), but there is no need to fear overcropping by the growers—this maximum is never met, let alone exceeded. The difficult terrain imposes its own natural limitations.

The vignerons of Côte Rôtie, as do those of Condrieu and Château Grillet, prune their vines in a characteristic manner: two or three plants, each on its own pole, are joined together at the top to form a sort of double triangle with the hillside as hypotenuse. Viewed from a distance, they create a picturesque silhouette, linked together in rows leading up and down the hillside.

When the young vines are planted, they are attached each to a single stick with rye straw. As the vines grow taller and bushier, two or three and sometimes as many as five of these sticks are joined together. The poles are reinforced near the bottom by smaller stakes.

This is done to steady the vines against the strong wind that sweeps down the Rhône Valley and buffets the vines. Some producers claim that this method of training also yields more grapes than training on single poles would.

Some trellis pruning—with the vines spread out on wires— is used on the hilltops, particularly on top of the Côte Brune. Some of the vines, though, are trained on single sticks, others in the same manner as on the hillsides. Some producers claim trellis pruning produces large yields.

The hilltops are, they say, not as good for the vine as the slopes, because the sun there is too strong. But Domaine Gerin, the largest holder of vineyards in Côte Rôtie, has produced some excellent wines, and for the most part, its holdings are on the top—which just goes to show that it's not what you have, but what you do with what you have that counts. Unfortunately, since 1969, its wine seems not to measure up to past standards.

Corn and fruit trees—apricots, apples, cherries, pears,

peaches—grow on the hilltops along with some vines, but relatively few.

Horses can be, and are, used to work the vineyards on top of the hills, but cannot be used on the precipitous terrain of the hillsides.

These hillsides have just the right exposure to insure maximum sunshine, which makes them also a great place to grow certain kinds of fruits and vegetables. The local early-ripening spring vegetables and fruits command high prices in the markets of Lyon. In some places radishes and lettuce can be seen interspersed among the vines.

The vineyards of Côte Rôtie cover approximately 172 acres (70 hectares) and yield nearly 52,920 gallons (2,000 hectoliters) in an average year. Most of the vineyards are in Ampuis. They extend from St.-Cyr-sur-Rhône in the north to Tupin-et-Semons in the south.

The vineyards are planted with the Syrah, locally called the Sérine or Sérene, and Viognier varieties. The Syrah grape yields a wine that is rough and coarse, requiring long aging in the bottle to round out and mellow. Up to 20% of the white variety, Viognier, is allowed by law to be used to soften the wine. At one time, both varieties were interspersed in the same vineyard, but the tendency today is to plant them separately.

There are fifty-four officially recognized vineyards or *quartiers* as they are called locally: Les Arches, Bassenon, La Blanchonne, Les Bonnevières, La Brocarde, Le Car, Chambretout, La Chatillonne, Les Chavaroches, La Chevalière, Chez Gaboulet, Chez Guéraud, Les Clos et La Claperonne, Le Cognet, Le Combard, Combe de Calon, Corps des Loups, La Côte Baudin, Le Cret, Fontgent, Le Fourvier, La Frizonne, Les Gagères, La Garde, Les Germines, La

Giroflarie, Grande Plantée et La Garelle, Les Grandes Places, Le Grand Taillé, Grosse Roche et La Balaiyat, La Guillambaude, Janville, Les Journaries, Lancement, La Landonne, Les Lézardes, Le Mollar, Montmain, Montuclas, Le Moulin, Les Moutonnes, Nève, Le Pavillon Rouge, La Pommière, Les Prunelles, Les Rochains, Rosier, Les Sévenières, Tharamon de Gron, Les Triottes, Le Truchet, La Turque, La Viallière, and La Viria.

Vineyard names rarely appear, though, on the labels of the Côte Rôtie wines. The best wines reputedly come from the twin slopes: Côte Brune and Côte Blonde.

Côte Brune, directly behind the village, has the darker soil, rich in schist (slatey rock), clay, and iron oxide. The lighter soil of Côte Blonde, slightly to the south of Ampuis, is made up of chalk, schist, clay, limestone, and flint. A small stream, Renard, separates the two slopes.

At one time these hills were owned by a nobleman, Maugiron. According to the legend, he gave the vineyards on these hills to his two daughters for their dowries. These two were as different as sisters could be. One daughter was a strong-willed and fiery beauty with olive skin and black hair; the other, gentle and amiable, was fair-skinned and blond. To the first he gave Côte Brune; to the latter, Côte Blonde.

As the story goes, the wines from the two vineyards took on the characteristics of their mistresses. The more full-bodied wines of Côte Brune are coarse and hard when young, requiring long aging to round out and soften. The Côte Blonde yields more delicate, quicker-maturing wines which also fade sooner.

It is said that the better wines come from the Côte Brune, that these wines have the most breed. But wines from either slope exclusively are difficult to find—they are usually blended together. The resultant wine seems to combine the best qualities of both. You will sometimes see a bottle of Côte Rôtie with "Brune et Blonde" on the label. Their different characteristics complement each other.

The other slopes to the north and south of the Brune and Blonde are not as highly regarded.

Côte Rôtie is a deep-colored red wine, big in body yet delicate and subtle. This aromatic wine has great finesse and character. Because it is rough and harsh in its youth, it should be allowed time to mature before being drunk. This wine begins to be palatable in its fifth or sixth year, and will continue to live, and improve, for a long time—decades.

With age the deep ruby of the Côte Rôtie fades to a garnet hue, and the nose takes on an aroma of raspberries. Some drinkers claim to detect the scent of violets, or even truffles.

With sufficient maturity Côte Rôtie develops sumptuous qualities—a big, distinctive bouquet and all the complexities expected of a great wine. On the palate it becomes full yet delicate, and velvety—truly one of the world's vinicultural treasures. These remarkably long-lived wines are the finest of the Côtes du Rhône region; they are surely the most complex and display the most finesse.

Appellation Contrôlée law requires that Côte Rôtie attain a minimum of 10% alcohol, but it usually ranges between 10.5% and 12%.

Côte Rôtie is a good accompaniment to red meats and game. In Ampuis they recommend it with small game, such as snipe. It sounds worth a try if you can find these birds.

Generally the harvest in Côte Rôtie begins about mid to late September, and goes on until mid October. The earliest harvest since World War II began on September 11, 1947; the latest, on October 15, 1956.

During the harvest the men carry the grapes in wicker

baskets on their backs to the top or to the bottom of the hill, which ever is closer. Those in the middle may take their choice.

The grapes are generally fermented in open cement, enamel, or wooden vats for eight to fifteen days, ten to twelve days on the average. The juice remains in contact with the skins, and the stems too, for the entire fermentation. Normally both varieties—Syrah and Viognier—are fermented together.

The wine is then aged in small oak or chestnut casks from two to three years.

M. Pierre Barge produces one of the few unblended Côte Brunes. He owns 3.7 acres (1.5 hectares) on that slope and none on the Côte Blonde. Viognier and Syrah are cultivated together in the vineyard. His yearly production is about 2,000 bottles; his average yield, 107 gallons/acre (10 hectoliters/hectare).

His wine is made up of 6% Viognier fermented in the same vat with the Syrah. He ferments his wine from eight to fifteen days in contact with the skins, ten to twelve days on the average.

M. Barge ages his wines in small oak (from the French Alps) casks for about three years. He says the wine needs at least five years, but reaches its peak from ten to twenty, depending on the vintage.

M. Georges Jasmin, who produced the finest wines I have tasted from Côte Rôtie, has vines on both Côte Brune (3.7 acres—1.5 hectares) and Côte Blonde (2.47 acres—1 hectare). His average yield is about 160 gallons/acre (15 hectoliters/hectare), producing about 5,000 bottles in an average year.

He uses 10% Viognier, and ferments his wine for at least ten days, and up to fifteen days—the average is twelve days—

on the skins. The wine is aged in small oak (from a forest near Burgundy) casks for an average of two years.

M. Jasmin likes his wine at six years of age, but says that it needs another four years to reach its peak. His '52 and '59, tasted in the summer of 1976, showed no signs of decline; the 1959 should continue to improve.

M. Dervieux, president of the Syndicat des Vignerons, owns 7.4 acres (3 hectares) and controls another 2.47 acres (1 hectare) on both Côte Brune and Côte Blonde. Presently he uses only 1% Viognier, but plans to increase this in the future because he says the Viognier adds to the bouquet of the wine, and the Syrah is too hard. His average production is 18,000 bottles, which works out to an average yield of about 364 gallons/acre (34 hectoliters/hectare).

Georges Vernay owns 2.47 acres (1 hectare) in Côte Rôtie averaging 214 gallons/acre (20 hectoliters/hectare). He ferments the juice with the skins submerged—sticks laid across the top hold the cap down—for three weeks in open wooden vats, leaving in the stems. This wine ages in small wooden casks for two years.

J. Vidal Fleury ferments its wine for ten to twenty days on the skins; twelve days is normal. The stems, too, are left in the open concrete vats during fermentation. Fleury uses the full 20% Viognier allowed by law. The wine is aged for at least two years in small French oak and chestnut casks. Better vintages are aged in these casks, or barrels, for up to three years.

M. Battier, of J. Vidal Fleury, says that its wines are drinkable at five years, but it takes an additional ten years for them to reach their peak.

There are approximately ninety growers in Côte Rôtie, not all of whom bottle their own wine. Most sell it to shippers such as Chapoutier, Jaboulet, Delas, and Fleury. Chapoutier owns 7.25 acres (3 hectares); Fleury, nearly 19.77 acres (8 hectares), making him the second-largest holder. Domaine Gerin, with the aid of American capital, is the largest holder with 24.7 acres (10 hectares); of this, 19.77 acres (8 hectares) are in production, 1.25 acres (.5 hectares) are on Côte Brune, none on Côte Blonde.

Côte Brune and Côte Blonde each cover about 29.65 acres (12 hectares), and each is divided among approximately ten growers. Fleury is the largest holder on the Côte Brune, with 6.6 acres (2.68 hecatres). Another 4.94 acres (2 hectares) are unplanted. M. Pierre Barge and M. Georges Jasmin each own 3.71 acres (1.5 hectares). The largest holder on Côte Blonde is, again, Fleury with 9.29 acres (3.76 hectares); M. Jasmin owns 2.47 acres (1 hectare).

Fleury owns nearly 3.71 additional acres (1.5 hectares) on the other slopes. It also buys grapes, making it the largest producer of Côte Rôtie wines.

Some others of the better-known producers: Jules Barge, André Bonnefond, Antoine Bonnefond, Claude Bonnefond, M. Cachet, Antoine Chambeyron, Marius Chambeyron, Christian Champagneux, Emile Champet, René Cluzel, Joseph Duplessy, André Gaston, Marius Gentaz, Marcel Gerin, Marcel Guigal, M. Pouzet, Jean Remiller, Société d'Exploitation Rhodanienne, and L. F. de Vallouit.

There is no cooperative in Côte Rôtie. The growers either bottle their own wine or sell it to the shippers.

The smaller growers work in their vineyards on weekends, assisted by family and friends.

Production of Côte Rôtie in 1975 totaled 38,843 gallons (1,468 hectoliters); 58,847 gallons (2,224 hectoliters) were produced in the previous year. 1973's production of 71,124 gallons (2,688 hectoliters) made it the most prolific vintage since the war.

Best years since World War II: 1971, 1969, 1949, 1947. Good years: 1970, 1967, 1966, 1964, 1961, 1959, 1955. Worst years: 1965, 1963, 1960.

An evaluation of recent vintages:

1975, 1974, 1973   Light, uneven wines that will be fast-maturing and not so long-lived. Of these three, 1973 is the lightest, and 1975 appears at this time to be the best. The best of these wines should turn out well.

1972   Some good wines were produced, and some not so good. Overall, this vintage, though fast-maturing, should last longer than the three that followed it.

1971   An altogether outstanding vintage that many producers consider in the same class as the great 1947s.

1970   Although not as highly regarded by the producers as '69 and '71, the wines have more finesse, at least at the moment. They won't be as long-lived as either of those other two.

1969   An excellent vintage which is in all respects the equal of 1971, and for some, even better. A great vintage.

1968   A light, uneven vintage which produced some worthwhile wines, but none of any interest is left.

1967, 1966   These two vintages were very good; '67 is more highly regarded, but the '66s should last longer. The better wines from both vintages aren't yet near their peak.

1965   One of the worst since the war.

1964   These wines are nearing maturity and can provide some pleasurable drinking now, but they will last.

1963   Whether 1963 or 1965 was the worse is hardly worth arguing about.

1962   Some very good wines that have been quite good for the past few years.

1961   Not so good as originally expected, but quite good nevertheless.

In the last century, horse-drawn barges were the only transport along the Rhône here. They made a stop near Ampuis to change the horses. The men took the chance to quench their thirst with the local wine. This helped to spread the name and fame of Côte Rôtie.

Chez René, a restaurant with one Michelin star, is not far from Côte Rôtie—across the river in St.-Romaine-en-Gal and just across the street from the excavations of the Roman city. The appetizers and desserts are excellent, but the cuisine falls down on the main courses; therefore, not worth the price.

5. CONDRIEU

South of Côte Rôtie, narrow granite terraces with low retaining walls—some dating from Roman times—climb up the slopes of steep hillsides.

Here are the vineyards of Condrieu. The ancients suggest that wine has been made here since about 58 BC. According to their writings a Helvetian tribe from the Swiss lowlands, ordered to Condrieu by Julius Caesar, planted vines here.

Martial described the wines, likening the perfume to the scent of violets.

It is thought that the Emperor Probus (276-282), who gets credit for recinding the edict of Domitian (AD 92) which prohibited the Gauls from cultivating the vine, had the Viognier plants brought to this area from Dalmatia.

In the fourteenth century the popes of Avignon drank the wine of Condrieu at their festivities.

Various modern writers have also sung its praises. Hugh Johnson describes Condrieu as having a "haunting floral scent like a faint and disturbing echo from the Rhine and a very long, rather spicy after-taste."

Waverley Root calls it the most seductive minor wine he has tasted.

The soil here is mostly granite mixed with some clay. Vines, bound to tall supporting poles with rye straw, are planted in the terraced vineyards up to altitudes of from 425 to 525 feet (130-160 meters). Only one variety of vine, the Viognier—known locally as Vionnier—is allowed for this AC.

Some 30.25 acres (12.25 hectares) of vines spanning seven villages and three departments are divided among nearly twenty growers. These villages, by department: Rhône (14.8 acres—6 hectares), Condrieu; Ardèche (.67 acre—.27 hectare), Limony; Lôire (14.8 acres—6 hectares), Chavanay, Malleval, St.-Michel-sur-Rhône (at one time known as St.-Michel-sous-Condrieu), St.-Pierre-de-Boeuf, and Vérin.

When Condrieu was granted an AC in 1940, only three villages were allowed to use this name: Condrieu, St-Michel, and Vérin. But because of the decline in plantings—a common situation in this region—the AC was extended to include four neighboring villages. The original three villages had 24.75 acres (10 hectares) under vines. But due to the abandonment of the more difficult portions of the vineyards, even with four additional villages the total plantings today add up to 30.32 acres (12.27 hectares).

The steepness of the slopes with the attendant difficulties of cultivation, is a major factor in the abandonment of many of the terraced vineyards.

During the war approximately one-third of the men were called away to fight leaving the women and children to take care of the vines. Consequently, the more difficult terrain was unworked, and left to the weeds and grass that soon overran it. This overgrowth of uncultivated terraces is unfortunately all too common in Côte Rôtie, St.-Joseph, and Cornas as well.

In addition to the problem of finding vineyard workers willing to do the back-breaking work required, there is another equally important one. The hillside land is worth three times as much for a homesite as it is for a vineyard. Consequently, houses may now be seen here scattered on the hillsides of Condrieu and its neighboring villages, while weeds and grass creep over the terraces.

Because of the small acreage and the difficult terrain very

little Condrieu' is being made. In 1975, 2,547 gallons (105 hectoliters) were produced. The maximum yield allowed by AC laws is 321 gallons/acre (30 hectoliters/hectare), but this is never met. Average production is half that amount. Of the recent vintages 1973 was the most prolific, with total production of 4,763 gallons (180 hectoliters). The fine 1970 vintage produced 3,704 gallons (140 hectoliters).

Most of the wine of Condrieu is made by the same men who grow the grapes. Only about 10% of the output is sold as grapes to shippers who make the wine and sell it. Delas is the most important shipper. From time to time Paul Jaboulet and J. Vidal Fleury buy grapes also.

Delas has recently planted a small vineyard in Condrieu, to help insure his supply of grapes.

Condrieu's largest and most important producer is M. Georges Vernay, who owns nearly half of the vineyards in Condrieu. He bottles *his* wines under two labels: Coteaux de Vernon and Condrieu. The Coteaux de Vernon vineyard is situated in a special site and reputedly produces the best wines of the area. Vernay's Condrieu label is used for all his other scattered vineyard holdings. In addition to his own vineyards, he also oversees nearly 2 acres (.8 hectare) of vineyards of the highly regarded Château du Rozay owned by Paul Multier. Vernay also markets Château du Rozay Condrieu.

M. Vernay ferments and ages his wines in American and Russian oak casks for six months. He says that Condrieu is best drunk very young, within one year, while it is at its fruitiest.

Other Condrieu producers of note: Antoine Cuilleron (Chavanay); Emile David (Verin); André Desormeaux (St.-Michel); Jean-Pierre Desormeaux (St.-Michel); Marc Dumazet (Limony); and Antoine Perret (Chavanay).

Condrieu is bottled in a Burgundy-style bottle. Though

the producers claim they had used a flute bottle for over a hundred years, they were forced to give it up in 1948. The Alsatian vintners were granted virtual exclusivity, by law, to the flute bottle. The vintners of Condrieu couldn't find any proof that it was the traditional bottle in that region, as it was in Alsace, so their claim to it was not recognized by the government officials who rule on such things. Today in France, Tavel, Alsace, and Château Grillet are allowed to use the flute bottle.

Condrieu is made basically in two styles. The traditional style is full-bodied and dry; the modern style, lighter and slightly sweeter. The newer style of wine may be slightly pétillant. In either case, the modern-style Condrieu is best when it is young and still has all its youthful fruity charm. The traditional-style Condrieu will age gracefully, developing into a wine with many nuances of flavor and bouquet.

Condrieu in either style is a golden-colored wine that ranges from medium dry to just off sweet. Its bouquet has floral, fruity overtones. Some experts say that the bouquet brings up the aroma of peaches; others, perhaps influenced by Martial, violets. An outstanding characteristic of the wine of Condrieu is its long spicy finish.

AC law decrees a minimum of 11% alcohol, but Condrieu is usually closer to 13%.

Condrieu is presented at its best served lightly chilled or at cellar temperature.

The modern-style Condrieu goes well with freshwater fish such as trout, perch, and pike. Local gourmets recommend it with *quenelles* and pike *au gratin*. The traditional-style Condrieu also goes well with scallops, conch, and shrimp.

Much of the production of Condrieu is sold to La Pyramide in Vienne and Beau Rivage in Condrieu, as well as other nearby restaurants.

The excellent Beau Rivage restaurant is a lovely place to enjoy the wine of Condrieu, either outside at the tables under the trees, or in the dining room. The service and food range from very good to outstanding. One wonders why the Michelin inspectors saw fit to give this fine restaurant only two stars in their guide. It surely deserves three stars (the highest rating). The restaurant is outstanding in all respects.

In Les Roches de Condrieu, across the river from Condrieu, is the Bellevue. It is a good hotel, but poor service and only mediocre to good cuisine make this not so good as a restaurant despite the view over the Rhône.

6. CHATEAU GRILLET

Within the region of Condrieu is a single 6-acre (2.5 hectare) estate entitled to its own appellation: Château Grillet. In fact Château Grillet was granted an *appellation d'origine* in 1936, some four years earlier than Condrieu. Its reputation goes back a long way.

The wine of Château Grillet was known in the middle of the seventeenth century. It is even possible that wine was made here as far back as Roman times. Remains have been found of a Roman villa 328 feet (100 meters) below the château.

The walled city of Vienne, just a few miles upstream, was a Roman colony which produced wine. Pliny, in about AD 60, sang the praises of the wine of Vienne. As the Romans made wine in neighboring Condrieu, it seems reasonable to suppose that they made wine here at Grillet too. The Romans are reputed to have picked out some of the most favored sites in Europe for vineyards. Perhaps this hillside, too, was first terraced by Roman laborers.

Château Grillet has been highly regarded at least since the eighteenth century. When Thomas Jefferson toured the Côtes du Rhône, he was told that this wine, Château Grillet, was the best around.

A. Jullien, in his *Topographie de tous les vignobles* (1816), wrote that Château Grillet produces a luscious white wine, high in alcohol, with a very pleasing flavor and pretty bouquet, which is one of the better ones of its type in France and preferred to Condrieu.

Prior to World War I the grapes were allowed to become overripe in order to produce a bigger, more alcoholic wine. This is no longer done. Nowadays the grapes are harvested at the peak of ripeness, and this is reflected in the well-balanced wine being made from them.

Some writers have reported that Château Grillet becomes *pétillant* in the spring, in sympathy with the budding vines. In mid-summer it becomes still again and remains so until the following spring. I've never encountered this phenomenon, and M. Canet, proprietor of Château Grillet, says that neither has he. It's apparently just one of the strange legends that seem to become associated with certain wines.

Twenty years ago, one cask of red wine, from the Syrah grape, was produced at Château Grillet. The wine, I'm told, was similar to a St.-Joseph, light to medium-bodied and fruity. It was only an experiment, though, and hasn't been done again.

The Viognier Dore vines at Château Grillet are planted in rocky granitic soil on narrow terraces, some wide enough for only one or two rows of vines. The slope of the hillside makes this one of the steepest vineyards in the area. The average age of the vines at Château Grillet is forty years old. The oldest were planted at about the turn of the century, making them about seventy-five years old. Their average yield, of 268 gallons/acre (25 hectoliters/hectare), is less than the 321 gallons/acre (30 hectoliters) allowed by law. *Appellation Contrôlée* specifies at least 11% alcohol. The Viognier Doré vine is found only in this area around Condrieu.

As in Côte Rôtie and Condrieu, the vines at Château Grillet are tied to tall sticks joined together sort of in the shape of a teepee. This is done to give stability to the plants, which are buffeted by strong winds. At one time three poles were joined here, but today only two. By planting the sticks deeper into the ground, they've found that two can give the necessary support, making cultivation easier.

The rows of vines are planted up and down on the hills and the terraces rather than across, which adds to the problem of erosion no doubt, but is necessary here due to the Mistral. This method of planting affords some protection from the strong winds by giving the vines less wind resistance.

The hillside vineyard, in terraced rows, curves like a Greco-Roman amphitheater above the château. These vines, facing due south, grow at altitudes from over 492 feet (150 meters) up to 820 feet (250 meters). Below the 492-foot altitude of the château there are more vines.

The château is in Vérin; the vineyard is in Vérin (about two-thirds) and St.-Michel-sur-Rhône (about one-third). Some parts of the vineyard have lain uncultivated since the First World War. Although some of these abandoned terraces still bear vines, they are no longer tended.

The work is very difficult on the steep hillsides and cannot be done by machines. The work must all be done by hand here. To spray the vines, the men must carry the heavy spray cans up and down the steep terraces. The stone to repair the crumbling terraces has to be carried up the slopes on the backs of the men. The granitic rock of the hillside, used to build the terraces, appears to be made up of tiny pebbles fused together from heat and pressure. In some places the terraces were hewn out of the living rock. The soft rock of the hillside is easily broken. Over the course of centuries, it has crumbled to provide the topsoil of the vineyard.

Now, because of the higher price commanded by Château

Grillet, additional parts of the vineyard are being cultivated again. If the entire property were planted, it would add another 1.25 acres (.5 hectare) to the vineyard.

A factory, built some forty years ago across the river and slightly to the south, attracts workers away from the vineyard. Château Grillet must pay industrial wages to the vineyard workers in order to compete. This, of course, also adds to the price of the wine.

Château Grillet has three men working full-time and some women working part-time.

Many people believe that Château Grillet's scarcity makes it expensive. While this surely adds to the price, the major factor has to be the high production costs of this fine wine.

The harvest generally begins in early October, give or take ten days.

The grapes are pressed in a compressed-air pump, and separated from the skins as quickly as possible. Fermentation takes place in 529-gallon (20-hectoliter) stainless steel and enamel vats. The wine is matured in small French oak casks. After two years in cask, the wine is bottled and put on sale.

Château Grillet uses a distinctive brown flute-shaped bottle. It is one of the few ACs to use this particular bottle. But it is not done to be different. Actually, this is the traditional shape and color of the old wine bottles of this area around Condrieu. In the château cellar there are some of the old hand-blown bottles from the last century. They are just a little taller and slenderer than the modern molded ones.

The flute bottle was used here for over one hundred years. Château Grillet almost lost the right to use this bottle when the wine laws ruled on the allowable shapes for some regions. Proof was found, though, in old invoices that this had been its traditional bottle, and so it won permission to continue using the flute bottle.

Since about 1930 the entire output of Château Grillet has been estate-bottled. Previously some of it was sold in cask, but now Château Grillet is sold only in bottle.

This estate has been in the Neyret Gachet family for 150 years. Today it is the property of M. André Canet and his wife who is a member of the Neyret Gachet family. The estate had been divided among three branches of the family, but when they had the opportunity, the Canets bought the entire estate, their hearts being in the vineyard.

Château Grillet is the smallest area with its own appellation in France. Production varies from 1,058 gallons (40 hectoliters), as in 1975, to the 2,117 gallons (80 hectoliters) of 1973, the highest since World War II.

In the 1950s most of the production of Château Grillet was sold to two restaurants, La Pyramide in Vienne and Beau Rivage in Condrieu. At that time the average output was about 2,000 bottles. Today it is 8,000 bottles. Consequently, Château Grillet can now be found in the U.S.A. and England as well as other countries outside of France.

The dry summer heat and mild autumn warmth usually allow the grapes at Château Grillet to ripen properly. M. Canet rates the most recent vintages as follows:

1975 Expected to be very fine (a very small harvest).
1974 Good.
1973 Lacked some of the body that is characteristic of this wine, but with more perfume (the largest vintage since the war).
1972 Good, a vintage of which M. Canet is very fond.
1970 Very fine.

This last wine, the 1970 Château Grillet, is one of the greatest bottles that I've had the pleasure of drinking. It was a spectacular wine, from its golden color to its fragrant perfume of flowers and spice and other things nice. It had an elegance and charm in the mouth and a long-lingering spicy finish to encourage us to sip and savor every drop.

M. Canet says that the wine improves with a half-hour of air. Mme. Canet notes that in the old days the wine was decanted—not just for taking it off the sediment (that it had in those days) but also for allowing the wine to develop with air. The extra contact with the air allows the bouquet of the wine to expand, to develop to its full potential. Château Grillet is best served chilled, but not too cold as this would destroy its fine bouquet.

The better vintages bear an oval label on the neck of the bottle which reads; Cuvée Renaissance. The 1970 bore this mark of distinction.

M. Canet feels that Château Grillet is at its best several months after bottling, but I prefer it with several years of maturity. The 1970 mentioned above was enjoyed in 1976.

Maurice Healy (*Stay Me with Flagons*) has written: "I once drank a Château Grillet that was over seventy years old, and delicious. . . . It had preserved its vinosity, and the clean, pebbly taste was quite remarkable. It seemed to leap the intervening hundred miles or more to link hands with Chablis, but it appeared to me to be of a majesty greater than that attained by Chablis, or any Burgundy except Montrachet."

Some writers have described Château Grillet as golden orange in color and with a bouquet of fresh oranges. These characterisitics escape me. I find Château Grillet to be a golden-colored wine with a fragrant floral perfume. Its full flavor makes it a fitting accompaniment to veal, pork, poultry, or fish.

M. Canet says that it goes very well also with cheese and desserts. He mentions a dessert of custard with pineapple that he was served and found to go remarkably well with his wine.

There doesn't seem to be any special significance to the name Grillet; probably it was the name of one of the earlier owners. As Maurice Healy so aptly put it, ". . . although the slope [Côte Rôtie] is roasted the château is not grilled."

7. ST.-JOSEPH

Just south of Condrieu are the vineyards of St.-Joseph. At one time these wines were known as Vin de Mauves. This had nothing to do with their color, which was decidedly not mauve! They were named for the little wine town of Mauve in this district. At another time they were called Vin de Tournon. Today the appellation takes its name from its most celebrated vineyard (*mas*): St.-Joseph.

Louis XII (1462-1515) owned a vineyard, Clos de Tournon, in this area. The town of Tournon boasts a castle and some fifteenth-century houses. Henry II and the poet Ronsard, in the sixteenth century, were known to have admired these wines.

Victor Hugo, writing in *Les Misérables* about M. Myriel's reception for Jean Valjean, says that besides the wine of Tournon, *vin ordinaire* was served because the Vin de Tournon was expensive.

The vines of St.-Joseph as in most of the vineyards of the northern Côtes du Rhône, are planted on the granite terraces of steep escarpments. The terraces are built of dry stone—without aid of mortar; the biggest stones are on the bottom of the walls which are then built up with progressively smaller rocks. Some of these terraces cling to precipitous hillsides rising 394 to 984 feet (120-300 meters) in altitude.

Cherry trees can be seen on the hillsides of St.-Joseph. There are also some apricot trees growing in the vineyards.

The trees provide some protection to the vines from the whipping winds of the Mistral.

Syrah vines for the red wines, and Marsanne and Roussanne for white are planted in sand and clay on narrow granite terraces. In some places the incline is so steep the terraces hold only one row of vines, but generally there are two or more rows. The growers use rye straw to bind the vines to the tall stakes that hold them up. The rye straw has been chosen because it doesn't break (it is wetted before tying) and is resistant to rain. Perhaps also in part because it is traditional. The growers prefer straw that has been harvested by hand.

Because of the steepness of these hillsides mechanization isn't possible. Although some work is done by mules, most of this difficult labor requires manpower. While Chapoutier has four full-time workers for his 66.7-acre (27-hectare) vineyard in Châteauneuf-du-Pape, he needs three men to work his St.-Joseph vineyard of only 14.8 acres (6 hectares).

The difficulty of cultivating these steep slopes and the extra expense involved has led, as in Condrieu and Côte Rôtie, to many terraces being abandoned. In some places entire terraced hillsides can be seen overgrown by weeds and grass.

The vineyards of St.-Joseph are well sheltered from the extremes of the weather, more so than those of neighboring Condrieu, for instance. Two olive trees, the northernmost olive trees in France, grow in a sheltered location in the Chapoutier vineyards.

When this AC was created in 1956, six towns were allowed to label their wines St.-Joseph. From north to south: Vion, Lemps, St.-Jean-de-Muzols, Tournon, Mauves, and Glun. In 1969 nearly two dozen additional towns were granted permission to call their wine St.-Joseph providing that they met the standards of this AC. Those in the Ardèche department (284 acres-115 hectares) besides those listed above are Ardoix, Arras-sur-Rhône, Audance, Champagne, Charmas, Châteaubourg, Félines, Guilherand, Limony, Ozon, Peyraud, St.-Désirat, St.-Etienne-de-Valoux, Sarras, Secheras, Serrières, and Talencieux. The towns in the more northerly Loire department (17 acres-7 hectares): Chavanay, Malleval, and St.-Pierre-de-Boeuf. These last three towns, along with Limony in the Ardèche, are allowed to label their white wines Condrieu if they are made from the Viognier grape and according to the other standards of that AC.

AC laws require a minimum of 10% alcohol and a limit of no more than 430 gallons per acre (40 hectoliters per hectare). This maximum imposes no problem for the approximately one hundred growers of St.-Joseph. In 1975, 51,440 gallons (1,945 hectoliters) of red and 6,455 gallons (245 hectoliters) of white were produced from 294 acres (122 hectares) of vineyards; 1974 production amounted to 97,850 gallons (3,700 hectoliters) of red and 16,195 gallons (610 hectoliters) of white. Average yields: 1975—190 gallons (20 hectoliters); 1974—380 gallons (35 hectoliters).

Some of the more noted producers and shippers: Chapoutier (Tain), Gérard Chaves (Tournon), Gustav Coursodon (Mauves), Delas (Tain), Emile Florentin (Mauves), Jean Desbos (St.-Jean-de-Muzols), Pierre Gonon (Mauves), Jean Louis Grippat (Tournon), Jean Minodier (Mauves), Ernest Trollat (St.-Jean-de-Muzols), Raymond Trollat (St.-Jean-de-Muzols), Paul Jaboulet (Tain), Jean Marsanne (Mauves), and Caves Co-op (Tain).

Red St.-Joseph is ruby in color with a strawberrylike perfume. It ranges from light to medium in body and is quite fruity. As it has some tannin, this wine will improve in bottle, although it won't live as long, or develop as well, as its neighbor across the river, Hermitage.

The quality of the vintage is similiar to that of Hermitage. (For vintage evaluation see Chapter 10, Hermitage.)

St.-Joseph is a good wine to drink with light meats such as pork, veal, and lamb. It will also complement turkey and mild cheeses.

The white St.-Joseph goes well with trout and other freshwater fish.

The Hostellerie Château de Châteaubourg, a restaurant in an old, beautifully renovated château, is a fine place to enjoy a meal of regional dishes accompanied by the local St.-Joseph.

8. CORNAS

South of Tournon and the vineyards of St.-Joseph, in the foothills of the Cevennes, are the vineyards of Cornas. Cornas, Celtic for "burnt earth," is a fitting name for these sun-drenched vineyards. Cornas has an unusual climate for the northern Côtes du Rhône. It seems more southern, with more of a Provençal climate, what with the olive, fig, and almond trees which flourish here.

The vineyards of Cornas, along with those of Côte Rôtie and Hermitage, are the oldest of the entire Côtes du Rhône. The wines of Cornas were mentioned by Martial, Ovid, and Pliny the Younger some 2,000 years ago.

Charlemagne is reputed to have stopped in Cornas and sampled the local wine.

In the tenth century the vineyards of Cornas came into the domain of the monks. Reference to these vineyards can be found in the register books (Cartulary) of St.-Chaffre-du-Monastier Abbey. And the tenth-century *Le Bref d'Obéd-ience* of Viviers Canonry contains this reference:

Galbertus tenet ecclesiam situm in Cornatico cum vinea et Campo.

Louis IX, known as Saint Louis, reportedly enjoyed the robust red wine of this area in the thirteenth century.

The vineyards of Cornas, continuing to enjoy favor, were extended in the fifteenth and sixteenth centuries.

More recently, the esteem in which Cornas wine was held was expressed by turn-of-the-century Burgundian shippers, who reputedly blended wine of Cornas into their Burgundies for color and body.

As is typical of the northern Côtes du Rhône, Syrah vines are grown here in stony granite soil on steeply terraced hillsides. These hillsides—some rising at a 45 degree angle—face south for maximum sunshine.

Though most vineyards of Cornas are planted on the hills, vines are also grown on the flats.

The chalky soil in the northern portion of Cornas might seem to be more suited to white wines. But only red wines may be labeled Cornas. And these reds must be 100% from the Syrah grape.

Some white wine is made in Cornas but it is entitled only to the regional Côtes du Rhône AC.

The regional AC, Côtes du Rhône, can be used for wines from approximately 130 villages and towns throughout the Côtes du Rhône region. Wine from specific villages having their own AC, such as Cornas, which fails to meet the more stringent standards of the local AC, can if it meets the regional AC requirements be labeled as simple Côtes du Rhône (AC) wine.

Because of the steepness of the hillsides, this difficult terrain must be cultivated by hand, back, and sweat of the brow. As in St.-Joseph and Hermitage, some animals are used. There are five or six horses and mules working in the vineyards of Cornas. A winch is used to haul the grapes to the hilltops during the harvest, which reduces some of the strain on the vineyard workers.

As in the rest of the northern Côtes du Rhône, it is expensive to cultivate and maintain the terraced vineyards in Cornas. Since 1949 about half the vineyards have been abandoned to be overgrown by weeds and grass. In the past few years, with the benefit of the higher prices now commanded by these wines, small amounts of reclamation and replanting have been done.

The Cornas vineyards spread over 185.3 acres (75 hectares). Production in 1975 amounted to 21,432 gallons (810 hectoliters), less than half that allowed by the AC laws; 1974 production was 41,965 gallons (1,586 hectoliters). AC specifies no more than 375 gallons/acre (35 hectoliters/hectare). Cornas must be at least 10.5% alcohol.

Generally the Syrah ferments in contact with the skins for about ten days. Twice a day, morning and evening, men push down the *chapeau* or "cap" (skins and stems pushed to the top of the fermenting vats by the violent action of fermentation). This results in a deeply colored red wine. Additional tannin is picked up from fermenting the wine with the stems of the grape bunches. This results in a slow-maturing wine. The wine is aged in oak casks for about one and a half years before bottling.

The wine of Cornas is similar to that of its northern neighbor across the river, Hermitage. Cornas, though, matures faster and doesn't live as long. A 1961 Jaboulet Cornas tasted in 1976, when it was fifteen years old, had reached maturity and showed no signs of going off with old age.

A young Cornas can be tannic and rough, but with sufficient age it can mature into a soft, round, and velvety wine with a distinction of its own. Cornas ranges from medium to deep ruby in color and its perfume is reminiscent of raspberries. This wine goes well with strong cheese, roast beef, and steaks.

There are some thirty growers in Cornas, which makes the average holding less than 5 acres (2 hectares) per grower. About half of these growers bottle their own wine. Most of the rest sell their product to shippers. Ten of them belong to the cooperative of Tain. Many of the small growers work the vineyards only on Sunday, being busy with a full-time job during the week. Some of the small producers who make their own wine keep it for themselves, their family and friends, and perhaps, sell a small amount to a few customers.

The largest shipper bottling the wine of Cornas is Delas, who also owns 12⅓-14¾ acres (5-6 hectares).

Verilac and Boissy-Delaygue are important shippers. Paul Jaboulet, too, bottles a good Cornas.

Two of the largest independent grower-producers in Cornas, with 12⅓-14¾ acres (5-6 hectares) each, are Auguste Clape and Joseph Michel et Fils.

Other respected producers include Guy de Barjac, Marcel Juge, Joseph Lionnet, Michel Lionnet, Marc Maurice, Louis Verset, Noël Verset, and Alain Voge.

St.-Joseph, Cornas, and St.-Péray have a local wine fraternity, La Confrérie des Chevaliers de la Syrah et Roussette—the brotherhood of Knights of the Syrah and Roussette (a subvariety of the Roussanne).

Local producers favor the wines of 1971, 1967, 1961, 1952, and 1949. Other good vintages: 1975, 1973, 1972, 1969, 1966, 1964, 1962, 1960, 1959, 1957, 1954. As elsewhere in the Côtes du Rhône, 1968 and 1963 were the worst years.

9. ST.-PERAY

St.-Péray, on the west bank of the Rhône, is just across the river from the city of Valence. This little wine town lies at the foot of the white stone crag of the Montagne de Crussol. The impressive ruins of Château de Crussol which crown the mountain stand over 500 feet above the plains below. This fortified castle, built in the twelfth century and in ruins since the seventeenth, dominates the landscape.

Local legend has it that when Napoleon was garrisoned at Valence in 1795, he risked his life to scale the cliff to reach the ruins at its summit.

The vineyards of St.-Péray are planted on narrow terraces rising up the steep hillsides behind the town.

Records indicate that the vineyards of St.-Péray were planted by the monks in the tenth century. But local producers believe that the Vinum Helviacum of Pliny and Plutarch was the wine of St.-Péray.

Henri IV (1553-1610) favored the still white wine of St.-Péray. And that indomitable German, Richard Wagner, ordered one hundred bottles of St.-Péray in a letter of December 2, 1877. At that time Wagner was busily at work on *Parsifal* (and perhaps needed some encouragement).

Up until the early nineteenth century St.-Péray was a still white wine—sometimes dry, sometimes sweet. Some old-timers say they can remember harvesting the grapes one by one, for a vintage struck by the "noble rot," *pourriture noble.* They say this still happens on occasion—both the attack of

83

pourriture noble and the hand harvesting of a berry at a time—but I've never met up with the sweet St.-Péray produced as a result.

In about 1823 M. Louis Alexandre Faure applied the champagne method, with the secondary fermentation in the bottle, to the still white wine of St.-Péray, to produce a sparkling wine, and was able to declare, like a latter-day Dom Pérignon, "I'm drinking stars."

Since 1929 most of the production of St.-Péray grapes has been made into *mousseux* (sparkling wine), always by the champagne method. St.-Péray Mousseux is fuller and fruitier than champagne, though, of course, not as elegant.

The difficult labor of the vineyard workers required to cultivate and maintain these steep vineyards is sometimes, but rarely, taken over by horses—mountain goats might be a better choice if they could be trained to harness.

Just the opposite of its northern neighbor, Cornas, the St.-Péray AC applies only to white wines, both still and sparkling, made from Marsanne and Roussette grapes. The Roussette is a new, improved variety of the Roussanne. Marsanne, a shy bearer, is planted on the lower slopes; Roussette vines dig their roots into the soil of the middle and upper slopes.

The soil here is made up of limestone and granite under a layer of stones and pebbles.

Only those St.-Péray wines made to sparkle by the champagne method are entitled to the AC St.-Péray Mousseux.

Though always the product of a single year, St.-Péray Mousseux is not vintage-dated.

The *mousseux* of St.-Péray is less subject to the vagaries of the weather than is the still wine. Some producers bottle a still white only in the better years. Unlike the *mousseux*, the still wine is vintage-dated.

There are some ninety growers in St.-Péray, owning 138 acres (56 hectares) of vines. The largest owner, with 19¾ acres (8 hectares), is M. Jean Chaboud. M. Pierre Darona, with almost the same amount, is a close second. Other notable producers include; Eugène Mathon, Michel Milliand, Jean Teyssere, Michel Viogeat, Auguste Clape, Coutelle, Fraisse, Pradon, and Vogue. These last five grower-producers have joined together, along with five others, to form a cooperative. This co-op is used only in the production of their *mousseux*; the still wine is made individually. Each producer labels part of the *mousseux* with his name and the rest with the name of the co-op, Cave Coopérative de Champagnisation de St.-Péray.

As with champagne, the still wine is bottled with the addition of a small amount of sugar solution and yeast. The yeast eats the sugar and causes a second fermentation to take place in the bottle. One of the by-products of the fermentation—carbon dioxide—is trapped in the wine, causing it to bubble, or sparkle, when the cork is popped and the bubbles of carbon dioxide rush to escape.

Fermentation creates another by-product, this one undesirable—sediment. The sediment has to be removed as it will make the wine cloudy when the carbon dioxide mixes it with the wine.

In order to separate this sediment from the wine it must first be gathered together neatly in a little pile in the neck of the bottle. The bottles of *mousseux* are placed in special racks called *pupitres*. These long racks are four rows high and six bottles wide.

A man called a *remueur* comes by each day to "riddle"

the bottles; he gives each bottle a slight twist, and repositions it in the rack at a slightly higher angle. Eventually the bottles are upside down and all the sediment is sitting on the temporary crown caps.

The next step is to expel the sediment—disgorgement. This is done by hand at the co-op, rather than by the more common method that involves freezing the neck of the bottle. This is a small cellar and not equipped with modern, expensive machinery. They are still using the old methods— not that their wines are any the worse for it, they might even be better.

The Union des Propriétaires of Tain has ten members in St.-Péray. Most of the St.-Péray wine made by this co-op is *mousseux*, but it does produce a small amount of still white. The entire process in producing the sparkling wine takes nine months. The first fermentation takes place at Tain, then the bottled wine returns to St.-Péray to be made into bubbly.

Verilhac, an important shipper, bottles his St.-Péray as Côte Vergne.

Coteau Gaillard is a highly regarded estate in St.-Péray.

Many old-timers here prefer the still white St.-Péray over the sparkling. But they seem to be in the minority since two-thirds of the wine of St.-Péray sparkles.

St.-Péray *mousseux*—both *brut* and *demi-sec*—is pale golden in color, the still wine is medium straw. Both are fruity, medium to full-bodied, and have a refreshing acidity. Some tasters claim to detect a scent of violets in the bouquet, but I find it more fruity than floral.

AC requires at least 10% alcohol. It also sets the maximum yield at 428 gallons/acre (40 hectoliters/hectare). Total production of St.-Péray in 1975 was 23,285 gallons (880 hectoliters); in 1974, 45,405 gallons (1,716 hectoliters).

To qualify for the AC, the grapes must come from St.-

Péray or a portion of the neighboring village of Toulaud. In addition, the *mousseux* must achieve its sparkle by secondary fermentation in the bottle, at St.-Péray or Toulaud.

St.-Péray, still or sparkling, is a good choice for accompanying the fruits of the sea. The still St.-Péray goes well with freshwater fish. Drink a toast to the wines of the Côtes du Rhône with the *brut mousseux* of St.-Péray.

In nearby Valence is the restaurant Pic, one of France's palaces of gastronomy awarded three stars by Michelin. It is a good place to dine if you like the show—the waiters go through all sorts of rituals, distracting if you're out to enjoy your company and the cuisine. The cuisine is outstanding however.

10. HERMITAGE

The vineyards of Tain owe their name, Hermitage or Ermitage, to the hilltop retreat of a legendary hermit. There are a number of versions to the hermit legend. I'll give you all the ones I've heard, and you can take your pick—whichever seems most likely, or most appealing to your sense of poetic interpretation.

Here is number one: Saint Patrick established the vineyards of Hermitage. Fleeing persecution, he arrived in the northern Rhône Valley where he sought refuge on the high hill above Tain. He was hungry and thirsty, but lacked both food and drink. Getting down on his knees, he sent up a prayer for help.

Angels came to the rescue—they planted vines, which miraculously bore ripe fruit overnight. *Voilà!* food (grapes) and drink (wine).

Or, if you prefer, an unknown person fleeing from the Roman conquerors found refuge and the answer to his prayers in the miracle of the vines, and he became our hermit.

Another legend, one with various twists of its own, tells us that a knight, Chevalier Henri Gaspard de Sterimberg, was the hermit of Hermitage hill. He had been seriously wounded in the crusade against the Albigensian heretics, and stopped to pray at the small chapel of St.-Christopher on the hill above Tain. (This chapel, today in ruins, stands among the vines on the site of a Roman temple to Hercules.) At prayer he had a vision, telling him to stay.

He sent an appeal to Queen Blanche de Castile to intercede for him. He had sought permission from the prior of the local abbey, St.-André-le-Bas (the abbey's claim to this chapel had been acknowledged by Pope Pascal in 1100), to build a shelter there. She aided the wounded knight in his appeal.

Sterimberg built a shelter and added to the vineyard near the chapel with vines that the monks gave him. He lived alone there and tended the vines of the hermitage until he died.

Or else—he was weary, not only with fighting, but world weary. In recognition for his bravery in the crusade, the queen of Castile, in a letter of May 12, 1225, granted him permission to plant a small vineyard on the St.-Christopher hillside.

Another twist to the Sterimberg legend says that he brought the vines with him from either Syracuse or Persia, where he had fought in the crusade against the Saracens.

But out of the misty realm of legend, and into the clear light of documented history, evidence indicates that the Romans grew wine here before the beginning of the Christian era. Roman mosaics, ceramics, and a store of forty amphorae have been found at Tain.

The Roman writers Pliny, Columella, Plutarch, and Martial all mention the wines of Hermitage—though, of course, not under its modern name.

Various accounts credit the Romans with importing the Syrah grape from Persia. Others credit the returning crusaders with introducing the Persian Shiraz—later changed to Syrah—to Tain.

The wine of Hermitage has been highly regarded since the early days. Poets and wine lovers have sung its praises.

The poet Boileau-Despréaux wrote in 1665:

> Un laquais effronté m'apporte un rouge bord
> D'un auvergnat fumeux qui, mêlé de lignage,
> Se vendait, chez Crénet, pour vin de l'Hermitage.

> An impudent lackey brings me a glass of red wine, brimful
> Of a heady *auvergnat* of mixed lineage,
> Which was sold at Crénet as a wine from Hermitage.

An insult to the taste of his master, who wasn't about to be fooled by such a miserable substitution.

In 1691, John Hervey, first Earl of Bristol, bought Hermitage Clarett (sic) and various Côtes du Rhône wines for his cellar. Hervey is reputed to have shown excellent taste in his choice of claret. He continued buying "Hermitage Clarett, Côte Rôty, and Condrieux" up until 1737.

In 1814 Beauvillier praised the red Hermitage. A. Jullien, around the same time, named the vineyard (*mas*) of Hermitage along with the vineyards of Lafite and Romanée-Conti as those producing the best red wines in the world. He listed in order of quality the following vineyards (*mas*): Méal, Gréfieux, Beaume, Raucoule, Muret, Guoignière, Bessas, Burges, and Lauds.

Sir Walter Scott, in his book *Charles le Téméraire* (1831), had a character remark: "I will eat a mouthful with you and I will win you over with a flask of old Ermitage."

Not only sought after in its own right, Hermitage was much in demand to fortify the finest clarets. Hermitage Clarett was often listed in cellar books and on lists put out by reputable wine merchants.

The letter books of Nathaniel Johnson, noted Bordeaux wine broker, show that the 1795 Lafite, with some Hermitage blended in, was the best-liked wine of that fine vintage. Hermitage was added only to the better clarets; Hermitage was not inexpensive.

Henderson, in the *History of Ancient and Modern Wines* (1824), wrote about the production of wines to be shipped to England: "To each hogshead of Bordeaux add three to four gallons of Spanish Alicante or Benecarlo or half a gallon of stum wine" (unfermented grape juice). This was to strengthen the delicate Bordeaux for the voyage. Sometimes, Henderson notes, a small quantity of Hermitage was used.

Noted wine authority André Simon says that he saw an invoice from the early 1830s of a highly respected merchant for Lafite Hermitagé ("Hermitaged").

In 1860, Cyrus Redding wrote that four-fifths of Hermitage was sold to Bordeaux to be used for "sophisticating Claret."

Belgium, the Scandinavian countries, and the Hanseatic cities of Germany liked their claret "Hermitaged." This was due, at least in part, to the colder climate of those countries. (And we all know that alcohol is the best warmer against that wintry chill.)

Adding Hermitage to claret was an accepted practice, openly declared. This was no dilution; this was an improvement.

One wit is reported to have remarked that the quality of the wine of Lafite was more dependent on the weather in the Rhône than in Bordeaux.

The highway between the Rhône river and the hills of the Côte was well frequented in the seventeenth century. In 1642, King Louis XIII passed along this route. At one point, due to the difficulty of passage, the king was transferred from his carriage to a sedan chair, and carried across the more dangerous sections.

Local publicity-minded vintners took advantage of the king's accessibility to offer him some of their best wines. At a rock jutting out onto the highway, King Louis stopped to have a small seventeen-course snack and some of the local wine. In his honor this rock is known as *la table du Roi*, the king's table.

In 1902, M. Loubet, president of France, was served Hermitage at the court of the Russian czars. He was told that this wine had been served at court since 1663, nearly 250 years.

Hermitage was a popular wine in nineteenth-century England. Professor George Saintsbury, in his classic *Notes on a Cellar Book* (1933), declared Hermitage the manliest French wine he had ever drunk. He added that the greatest vintage he had known was either an 1846 Hermitage (drunk when it was forty years old) or an 1858 Romanée-Conti.

Rising approximately 980 feet (300 meters) above Tain, the hill of Hermitage is very steep and picturesque. Rows of vines line the steps of the terraces. Here and there on rocky outcroppings are signs proudly naming the owner of this or that particular vineyard. Some of the terraces here, too, have been abandoned and not replanted.

On a good day you can see from the hill the beginning of the Alps, the Vercors foothills 18 miles (30 kilometers) away. There are apricot trees in some of the vineyards—apricots grow well in the same dry, sunny conditions as the vine. The trees provide protection for the vines. Down below are patches of yellow here and there—wheat fields. (During the phylloxera disaster, wheat and potatoes were planted as substitute crops in place of the devastated vines.)

The vineyards of Hermitage are in the crook of the

Rhône as it rounds the bend at Tain-l'Hermitage and
Tournon, below St.-Joseph. Spanning the Rhône and con-
necting the twin towns of Tournon on the west bank and
Tain on the east bank is the world's first modern suspension
bridge. It is now a pedestrian bridge, closed to motor
vehicles.

Slightly downstream is a newer bridge for vehicle traffic
built in 1826 by Marc Seguin, and reputedly an inspiration to
John Roebling, who designed the Brooklyn Bridge half a
century later.

The hill of Hermitage is just over 6 miles from the 45th
parallel, just halfway between the pole and the equator. It
has a southwesterly exposure. Consequently, the climate is
relatively warm, but not hot, although the sun does shine
brightly. The vines are planted for maximum sunshine. The
weather is fairly constant here. When it rains, the brisk wind
of the Mistral dries off the excess moisture.

Stone walls separate the different vineyards or parcels
(*mas*), from each other. At one time unblended wines from
single vineyards were produced, but this is rarely, if ever,
done today. The tendency is to combine grapes from the
various vineyards, fermenting, aging, and bottling them
together as a single wine.

The principal vineyards are Bessards at the top of the hill,
Méal in the middle, and Griffiaux toward the bottom. The
hill is part of the Massif Central. The soil of Bessards and
Méal is granite with rocks and pebbles. This soil is well suited
to the red Syrah plant. Griffiaux, with the richest soil—loess
and limestone—is better suited to the white varieties Marsanne and Roussanne.

Overall, the soil is very poor, but well drained. This is
advantageous for the vine, causing it to dig deep for
nourishment. The deeper the roots, the more constant the

environment of the plant. The roots of the vines go down 5-6.5 feet (1.5-2 meters) deep at the foot of the hill; at the top, far less, because of the rock.

Peleat and Racoules are part of Griffieux. Les Diognières is at the bottom, on a slight slope. Besides the vineyards mentioned above, others include La Croix, L'Homme, La Pierrelle, La Maison Blanche, L'Hermite, and La Varogne.

Chante Alouette ("song of the lark"), the most highly regarded white wine vineyard today, is part of Méal. Its soil is rocky, with granite and some clay. Chante Alouette is actually a white wine vineyard within a red wine zone. Chante Alouette is also a trade name of Chapoutier, the largest producer of Hermitage. Chapoutier, who is the sole owner of Chante Alouette, produces a white Hermitage from this vineyard and the area immediately surrounding it.

Hermitage hill is about 1.8 miles (3 kilometers) long and .6 mile (1 kilometer) wide. Vineyards cover 304 acres (123 hectares) of the hill facing south to southwest. Most of the vineyards are in Tain, with small portions in Crozes, Gervans, Erôme, and Larnage.

There are eighteen vineyards, locally called *mas*, recognized by French law: Beaumes, originally Beaume (white); Bessards (red); Croix (red); Croix de Jamanot (red); Diognières (red); Diognières et Torras (red); Les Griffieux, originally Gréfieux (red); Gros des Vignes (red); L'Hermite or L'Ermite (red); L'Homme (red); Maison Blanche (white); Le Méal (red); Les Murets, originally Muret (red and white); Peleat (red); Pierrelle (red); Les Racoules, originally Raucoule (red and white); Signaux (red); Varogne (red).

Other vineyards, subsections of the officially recognized vineyards, or brand names found on labels, are Burge (red); Chante Alouette (white); Chapelle (red and white); Columbiers (red); Guoignière (listed in Jullien); Lauds (listed in Jullien); Sizer (red); Sizeranne (red).

Chapoutier, a grower since 1808, is the largest owner of vineyards on Hermitage hill, with 76.6 acres (31 hectares). The members of the Propriétaires de l'Union Co-op, Tain, are the second largest, followed by Paul Jaboulet Aîné and Delas Frères. Rouchette, another notable name in these parts, is part of the Chapoutier empire. Gérard Chave, the area's oldest grower (since 1481)—that's the company, now, not the man—and quite possibly the best producer, is fifth with 19.8 acres (8 hectares), half in red and half in white. These five among them own 247.1 acres (100 hectares), leaving fifty-five to sixty others to divide the remaining 56.8 acres (23 hectares).

Some other noteworthy producers are Henri Sorrel, Jean Louis Grippat, Lord Gray-Terence, Jean et Michel Ferration, and Domaine de l'Hermite. Du Bourg is a reputable shipper, as are Delas and J. Vidal Fleury. Jaboulet's Le Chevalier de Sterimberg (white Hermitage), while not usually the equal of Chante Alouette, is still one of the finest white Hermitages produced.

The distance between vines in the vineyards here varies from 3.3 x 3.3 feet (1 x 1 meters) on the upper slopes to 3.9 x 4.3 feet (1.2 x 1.3 meters) lower down. Manual cultivation is used on the upper slopes. The lower slopes can be, and often are worked by mules, horses, and small tractors. Chapoutier uses mules, Chave, a horse. At the very top, where it is flat, mules, horses, and tractors are also used.

Heavy rains wash the soil down the hill and men must carry it back up in baskets on their backs, or, less romantic but easier on the men, on mules or horses—or even better, with the use of a winch. (That's winch, with an *i*, not an *e*.

Though, during the war there may have been some wenches struggling to carry up the eroded soil, what with the men away fighting.)

The top of the hill is entitled only to the Crozes-Hermitage appellation. Orchards of fruit trees, especially apricots, alternate with vineyards on the hilltop.

The vines in Hermitage are tied to stakes with rye straw, the traditional method of training the vines on the slopes of ti.c northern Côtes du Rhône.

Some 80% of the vines are the red grape Syrah. There are three varieties of Syrah, according to M. Chapoutier. Petite Syrah, the one with the smallest berries, is considered the best. This is the variety grown in the northern Côtes du Rhône.

The remainder is mostly the white Marsanne with some, but very little, Roussanne. The Roussanne variety is being used less and less. Because of its tendency to oxidize easily it has fallen out of favor and is being replaced with Marsanne plants.

At one time red and white grapevines were interspersed in the same vineyard, but they are planted separately today. This simplifies the harvesting, as the grape varieties ripen at different times.

Normally the harvest begins here between September 20 and October 10—the Syrah is a relatively early ripener.

The maximum yield allowed by AC law in Hermitage for all varieties is 428 gallons/acre (40 hectoliters/hectare).

Normally 100% Syrah is used to make the red Hermitage, although the white Marsanne and Roussanne varieties can be added, up to 15%. It had become traditional here to blend in white grapes in years when there was an overabundance of the white, and the wine laws for Hermitage have been amended to allow this blending.

Chapoutier says he never blends any white varieties into his red Hermitage. Chave normally blends in 2 to 3% of white because he feels it adds some finesse. It is certainly less common to blend in white grapes in Hermitage than it is in Côte Rôtie.

The grapes are crushed, and the red wine ferments in contact with the skins for at least two weeks, perhaps as long as three, in open wood, or closed concrete, vats. Chave ferments his wine for three to four weeks on the skins and with the stems, which are not separated out.

It's not as common as it used to be, but both Chapoutier and Chave use *foulage à pied* (treading by foot) to push down the cap of skins, stems, etc., into the fermenting must. (M. Chave says this is the way it is usually done in Mauve, Cornas, and perhaps other neighboring villages.) Twice a day, morning and evening, the men, between wooden poles placed across the open vat, "dance on the cap" to push it down. This doesn't break the cap apart; it keeps it together, and is supposed to be the best method. But one suspects that tradition is also a factor.

The red grapes (except for Chave's) are de-stemmed; white Hermitage is pressed and separated from the skins immediately. This wine is fermented in steel and enamel vats. Some producers, notably Jaboulet and Chave, ferment their whites for one month at cool temperatures, helping to retain all the fruitiness and freshness in the wine.

According to Allen Taylor (*What Everybody Wants to Know About Wine*, 1934), in Hermitage a bit of boiled wine was added to the freshly fermented must. This addition of concentrated wine would increase the alcoholic content; it is a form of chaptalization. This practice has reputedly been abandoned today. But producers are allowed to chaptalize by adding sugar to the must before fermentation to bring up the alcoholic content to the AC minimum. In poor years when the grapes don't get enough sunshine to ripen fully, they don't have enough natural sugar to produce a wine of 10% alcohol.

Chave ages his white for six months in wood, his red for nineteen months in small French oak casks. Chapoutier keeps his reds three years in wood, oak, and chestnut.

It used to be that the wine barrels and casks were made in house at the larger firms, such as Chapoutier, who employed their own coopers. Chapoutier still has one cooper working for it. He is kept busy making repairs to the old barrels now and doesn't have much time for making new ones.

Coopering is dying out as a trade; the cooper's tools are no longer even being made. Old ones have to be found. They are handed down from cooper to cooper—the same tools as used in the Middle Ages.

It takes an experienced cooper nine to ten hours to make one 52-gallon (2-hectoliter) barrel. So it is easy to see why handmade barrels are becoming a thing of the past. Machine-made barrels may not be so fine, but they are certainly cheaper.

Both chestnut and oak, according to Chapoutier, have very similar properties—much tannin, as well as imparting similiar flavors and aromatic characteristics to the wine. He says that chestnut is used more commonly because it is considerably less expensive—one-third the price of oak.

Red Hermitage has a good deep color. Some writers have described its qualities as portlike, without the brandy (the famous wine of Oporto being fortified by the addition of brandy). The only similarity to port that I can see is the heavy sediment it throws as it matures. Hermitage is rich in flavor, but it lacks the sweetness of port.

The bouquet of Hermitage is intense, spicy, and raspberrylike—some connoisseurs suggest wild raspberries. Others claim to detect wallflowers, iris root, and hawthorn. With age this intense bouquet becomes penetrating.

Although not high in alcohol (minimum is 10%), this wine is quite robust. It is harsh and tannic when young, but develops sumptuous qualities with maturity.

Hermitage is a slow-maturing wine needing at least six or eight years in bottle to soften, and fifteen or twenty will rarely hurt it. Red Hermitage is, reputedly, one of the longest-lived of all wines. The 1942 tasted in Chave's cellar was remarkable in 1976.

M. Chave says, however, that his red Hermitage is drinkable at two years, but is much better after five. He says the older wine can be opened for a whole day, and should have at least a couple of hours of air.

Being a full-flavored wine, Hermitage requires full-flavored meats, such as game, or strong cheeses to stand up to it and match it. I personally enjoy it with venison. M. Chave likes to drink his red Hermitage with woodcock or snipe.

Toward the end of the eighteenth century, white Hermitage was preferred to the red. Jullien said that Raucoule produced the best whites of Hermitage.

Cyrus Redding, in his *History of Modern Wines* (1876), called white Hermitage "the finest white wine France produces," and exclaimed that the real white Hermitage will keep for a hundred years "without the least deterioration."

I've heard stories of fifty-year-old whites that showed no signs of age. A 1952 tasted in M. Chave's cellar in 1976 was still young and fresh. Its only sign of age, or maturity, was its deep golden color. M. Chapoutier speaks of a 1929 Chante Alouette tasted in May 1976 which was still quite good.

White Hermitage is full, dry, and fruity. It has a bouquet that some have described as bringing up honeysuckle, but I have never noted this resemblance. I tend to agree with those who liken the aroma to gunflint. The better white Hermitages need at least five years of age to be really enjoyable, and fifteen won't hurt them. Some producers are making Hermitages to be ready sooner. These wines won't live as long.

White Hermitage goes well with pork and turkey. M. Chave likes his white Hermitage, a younger one, with *charcuterie*. With truffled *pâté* or the like he prefers an older white, even fifteen to twenty years old.

The only defect of the white Hermitage, perhaps, is that it is sometimes, especially in sunnier years, a little low in acidity. This causes the wine to seem somewhat awkward, or unbalanced.

Approximately two-thirds of the Hermitage produced is red. In 1975, 35,959 gallons (1,359 hectoliters) of red and 17,543 gallons (663 hectliters) of white were produced; in 1974, 63,478 gallons (2,399 hectoliters) of red and 38,632 gallons (1,460 hectoliters) of white.

AC law also allows the vintners of Hermitage to make a *vin de paille*, a "straw wine," under the Hermitage, or Ermitage, name.

This wine is quite rare and expensive today. It costs three to four times as much to produce as a regular white Hermitage. A big factor is the much reduced quantity of wine produced by the grapes.

Following the regular harvest, Marsanne and Roussanne grapes are laid out on straw mats—hence "straw wine"—to dry and shrivel up. This makes the grapes richer and more concentrated.

The grapes are then pressed, and the juice collected in small barrels to ferment. Fermentation proceeds very slowly due to the thickness of the must. The wine is then left to age for two to three years in small casks before bottling.

The only recent *vin de paille* that I know of is the one made by Chave. He produced one from the 1975 vintage—the first straw wine made by the Chave family in fifty years, since his grandfather used to make it.

M. Chave harvested his grapes at the end of September and left them on straw mats for two months to dry. At the end of November, the grapes were pressed, and the must fermented for eight to nine months.

This wine, when tasted in the summer of 1976, was a deep golden color, and had a rich, expansive aroma and full rich flavor. The sweetness was balanced by its acidity. With sufficient maturity, this wine should be a beauty. Chave expects to keep it for his own consumption because of the high price he would have to ask for it.

AC requires at least 14% alcohol for this wine, and sets a maximum of 300 gallons/acre (28 hectoliters/hectare).

Cyrus Redding also mentioned *vin de paille*. He said that very little of it was made because its price was very high. And, further, that this wine was not often successful.

Recent vintages, an evaluation:

1975   Uneven, ranging from fair to good. These wines should mature early and decline shortly afterward.

1974   Uneven, as with 1975, but perhaps the best of the three years from 1973 to 1975; fast-maturing.

1973   Uneven; similar to 1974 and 1975; these wines will mature soon and not live long. Some good whites were made.

1972   Excellent, slow-maturing wines from a much underrated vintage. Though some wines didn't live up to the vintage.

1971 An exceptional vintage; these wines will live longer than the 1970s. Most producers rate this as the best of the '69-'70-'71s. Only time will tell, but I'll go with the '70s.

1970 Outstanding, better than rated by the local producers. Will be ready sooner than the '69s and not be as long-lived.

1969 Very good to great wines, slow-maturing and long-lived; a year to cellar. Many producers rate this vintage higher than 1970, and they might be better in the end.

1968 In the same rotten class as 1963.

1967 Though not as highly regarded as 1966, some producers made better wines; some can be drunk now, and many will last well and go on improving.

1966 Very good. Some great wines were produced; these wines are continuing to improve.

1965 Mediocre; nothing worthwhile left.

1964 Very good wines without much staying power, quite enjoyable now.

1963 Very poor, among the two worst since World War II.

1962 Outstanding, will age.

1961 Exceptional to very great, still improving.

Older vintages: 1947, 1949, and 1952 were outstanding vintages; 1953, 1955, 1957, and 1959 were very good to excellent. All of these wines have held up very well and show no signs of going off.

An interesting development in Hermitage is the introduction of nonvintage wines that are blends of various years.

Chapoutier introduced his Grand Cuvée for sale, in France only, in 1965. His goal is to achieve an even quality from one year to the next. These wines are, surprisingly, more expensive than his vintage-dated wines. This, M. Chapoutier explains, is because he selects only his best wines for his Grand Cuvée blends. The bottling date is noted on the label.

Chapoutier's Grand Cuvée Hermitage is a blend not only of wines of different vintages, but also of different vineyards (*mas*)—approximately one-third each from Griffieux, Bessards, and Méal.

Chapoutier also bottles wines from special vats, in very small quantities. The numbered bottles represent a special selection of Grand Cuvée wines. They are not produced every year. In fact, Chapoutier has bottled only three special vats in the past decade.

J. Vidal Fleury also produces a vintage blend, labeled Grande Réserve.

This development has its supporters. They argue that it is done in Champagne, and the net result is not only more consistent wines but also wines of higher average quality. It is debatable. I rather like the variation from vintage to vintage myself. I think it makes wine drinking all the more interesting.

11. CROZES-HERMITAGE

The vineyards of Crozes-Hermitage curve around those of Hermitage, to the north, east, and south of the hill of the hermit. These vineyards, named for the tiny old town of Crozes-Hermitage, north of the hill and inland from the river, practically surround the hill and also cover part of the top. The vineyards of Crozes-Hermitage cover 1,359 acres (550 hectares) stretching across portions of eleven villages: Beaumont-Monteux, Chanos-Curson, Crozes-Hermitage, Erôme, Gervans, Larnàge, Mercurol, Pont-d-l'Isère, La Roche-de-Glun, Serves, and Tain-l'Hermitage.

Crozes-Hermitage, like its more celebrated neighbor Hermitage, produces both red and white wines. The white is the product of Marsanne and Roussanne grapes. The red is usually from 100% Syrah, but as in Hermitage, 15% of the white Marsanne and Roussanne varieties may be blended in.

At least one noted wine writer, Creighton Churchill, lists Grenache as the principal grape variety of Crozes-Hermitage! There is no Grenache grown in these parts, and none is allowed by law in these wines.

Production in 1975 of the red Crozes-Hermitage was 441,300 gallons (16,678 hectoliters). In 1974, 513,298 gallons (19,399 hectoliters) were produced. White Crozes-Hermitage production is considerably less: 1975, 28,312 gallons (1,070 hectoliters) and 1974, 43,527 gallons (1,645 hecoliters).

Yields in Crozes are limited to 428 gallons/acre (40 hectoliters/hectare) or less.

Crozes-Hermitage is fermented on the skins, nearly as long as Hermitage—from fourteen to eighteen days—but the resultant wine is less tannic, quicker-maturing, and not as long-lived.

As with Hermitage, it must achieve no less than 10% alcohol and chaptalization is permitted. This presents an interesting problem as far as declassification is concerned. Crozes-Hermitage and Hermitage may be declassified as a Côtes du Rhône only if the higher minimum alcoholic content for Côtes du Rhône, 11%, is achieved and there has been no chaptalization, as chaptalization is not allowed for AC Côtes du Rhône wines.

The fact that the producers here are allowed to chaptalize their wines to achieve the required 10% alcoholic content is explained by the more northerly climate of Hermitage and Crozes-Hermitage. The grapes here don't ripen as fully and develop as much sugar as in the vineyards to the south. In Côte Rôtie, too, the wine may be chaptalized. And their minimum alcohol is also 10%. Along with St.-Joseph and St.-Péray these wines have the lowest minimum alcoholic content in the entire Côtes du Rhône. Chaptalization is not, however, permitted in St.-Joseph or St.-Péray.

Four hundred growers in Crozes-Hermitage belong to the cooperative in Tain-l'Hermitage, comprising nearly two-thirds of the 665 members of this union of growers.

This Union des Propriétaires controls, in total, 1,236 acres (500 hectares), not all in Crozes-Hermitage. The membership list is broken down thus: Crozes-Hermitage—four hundred growers, Hermitage—fifteen growers, St.-Joseph—thirty growers, Cornas and St.-Péray—ten each, and two hundred growers of *vin ordinaire.*

This union is the only true cooperative in the northern Côtes du Rhône. There is a cooperative cellar in St.-Péray but each grower-producer who belongs to that co-op makes his own wine. The members combined their resources in order to afford better equipment to make their sparkling wine (*mousseux*). The Union des Propriétaires in Tain makes all the wine and ages, bottles, labels, and markets it under the co-op name.

Some fine Crozes-Hermitages are produced by the firms of Chapoutier (Les Meysonniers, red), and Paul Jaboulet Aîné (Domaine de Thalabert, red; La Mule Blanche, white). Raymone Roure, Jules Fayolle, Robert Michelas, and A. Serves Begot are highly regarded producers.

The wines of Crozes-Hermitage—both the red and white—are coarser and less distinctive than those of Hermitage. They have a slight taste of the soil.

The whites have been described by some as having an aroma of hazelnuts. They are dry and quite austere, but perhaps a little low in acidity. They go well with fish and chicken dishes in sauces.

The red wines require a few years in bottle to soften. Their aroma has been likened to wild hawthorn and raspberries. These wines are light- to medium-bodied and quite fruity and soft on the palate when mature. Red Crozes-Hermitage is a good choice to accompany a dinner of lamb or roast beef.

Generally, being not as highly regarded as Hermitage, these wines are quite reasonably priced. As they are faster-maturing, they offer a reasonable alternative to the long-lived Hermitage. Though they are not capable of achieving the heights of the Hermitage, they are, between their third and fifth year, perhaps, more enjoyable, as they are quite mature then and the better wines of Hermitage are still harsh and closed in.

(For an evaluation of vintages see Chapter 10, Hermitage.)

In 1846 the tasting committee of the Lyons Vinicultural Congress pronounced the judgment that Crozes-Hermitage resembled Hermitage so much that if these wines weren't brothers, then they were first cousins.

THE SOUTHERN
COTES DU RHONE

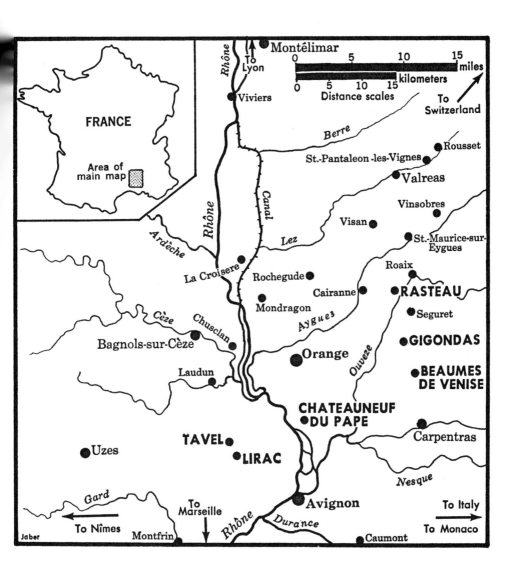

FRANCE

Area of
main map

Rhône

To
Lyon

Montélimar

0   5   10   15 miles
0   5   10   15 kilometers
Distance scales

To
Switzerland

Viviers

Berre

Rousset

St.-Pantaleon-les-Vignes

Valreas

Vinsobres

Visan

St.-Maurice-sur-Eygues

Lez

Roaix

Rhône

Canal

Ardèche

La Croisere

Rochegude

Cairanne

RASTEAU

Mondragon

Aygues

Seguret

Cèze

Chusclan

GIGONDAS

Bagnols-sur-Cèze

Ouveze

Orange

BEAUMES
DE VENISE

Laudun

CHATEAUNEUF
DU PAPE

Carpentras

Uzes

TAVEL

LIRAC

Nesque

Gard

To
Marseille

Avignon

To Italy

To Nîmes

Montfrin

Rhône

Durance

To Monaco

Jaber

Caumont

12. RASTEAU

There is some speculation that the Gauls made wine in the area around Rasteau before the Romans, but there seems to be little proof of it. Nor is there much to support the view that the Romans made wine here, although this is more likely. Vaison-la-Romaine, a Roman city built in the pre-Christian era, has been unearthed nearby. And given the suitability of this area to the cultivation of the vine, it seems possible that the Romans grew grapes and made wine here.

We know that wine has been made at Rasteau for a very long time, but the sweet fortified Rasteau *vin doux* is a comparative newcomer here, having made its debut only around 1930. At that time, M. Galabert, a native of the Pyrenees, was in charge of vinification at the co-op. As the harvest was being brought in, he noticed that many of the grapes were overripe. He was reminded of the overripe grapes used to make the sweet wine of the Pyrenees, and suggested to the growers that they make a *vin doux* at Rasteau. They went to the mayor of Rasteau with the idea, asking him to seek permission to make the *vin doux* from the prime minister of France—official permission being required before they could offer this new style of wine for sale under the Rasteau name. The prime minister granted them the right to produce the *vin doux*. And they have made one, weather permitting, ever since.

French AC laws acknowledge two types of fortified wines, but only one of them is considered a true fortified wine. Both

111

vin doux naturel and *vin de liqueur* are fortified by the addition of pure alcohol or brandy. The difference is in how—or more specifically, when—it is done.

With *vin de liqueur* (VDL), the fortifying spirit is added before fermentation. Consequently, the grape juice and spirit are fermented together. So *vin de liqueur* is classified by AC law as a sweet natural wine, not a fortified wine.

Vin doux naturel (VDN) is fortified by the addition of pure alcohol, at least 90 proof, from 5 to 10% by volume during fermentation. This brings up the alcohol level, which arrests the fermentation process. It also leaves the sugar not yet converted into alcohol in the wine, making a sweet (*doux*) wine. Both *vin doux naturel* and the *vin de liqueur* can be fortified with any type of pure alcohol, of at least 90 proof, but generally the local marc (brandy distilled from the skins, seeds, and pulp remaining after the grapes are pressed) is used.

To qualify for the VDN classification, AC specifies that the wine must be made from at least 90% of a single grape variety, or else a blend of Muscat, Grenache, Maccabéo, and/or Malvoisie.

Wines with the Rasteau AC may be either *vins doux naturels* or *vins de liqueur*. The VDN, though, is considerably more common.

Rasteau VDN and VDL are produced around the town of Rasteau in the Ouvèze Valley northeast of Avignon. The vineyards lie between the Aygues and Ouvèze rivers, in land around the town of Rasteau and the nearby villages of Sablet and Cairanne. Cairanne also produces a *vin doux naturel* under the name Cairanne VDN, but unlike the Rasteau, it is not an AC wine.

Grenache vines are planted in marl and gravel soil on the

slopes of the hills. The soil of the upper slopes is also mixed with clay; on the lower slopes it is mostly rocks and pebbles. It is forbidden to plant fruit trees, except olive trees, in the vineyards here.

The wine must be at least 90% from the Grenache. The other grape varieties used here are Clairette and Carignane, but any of the varieties allowed for Côtes du Rhône wines, up to 10%, may also be used. The vines must be four years old for the grapes to be used for the AC wine.

Rasteau comprises some 1,853 acres (750 hectares) of vines, but only about 371 acres (150 hectares) can be used to produce the VDN or VDL.

Though Rasteau VDN must achieve at least 14% potential natural alcohol, it usually ranges between 16% and 18%. Fortification increases the total richness to 21.5%—of this, at least 15% must be actual alcohol. The total richness is the actual alcohol plus the potential alcohol, or unfermented sugar. The VDL must attain naturally a minimum potential alcoholic level of 13%. When finished, it too reaches 21.5% total richness, with no less than 15% actual alcohol.

Rasteau VDN or VDL can be red, white, or rosé. White VDN, the most common, goes well with dessert, by itself as an aperitif, or over melon as an appetizer. Red VDN, which is drier than the white, is best sipped alone as an aperitif. Either red or white would go well with nuts, though this seems to be a novel idea in Rasteau, where they apparently don't munch on nuts. Both wines are best served cool, not cold.

Rasteau VDN white is light amber in color with a nutty (walnutlike), slightly rancid aroma. The flavor has undertones of vanilla, and though sweet to the taste, is balanced with sufficient acidity so that it isn't cloying. It finishes on a dry note. The red VDN, too, has a slightly rancid aroma underlying its more forward nuttiness. It is drier but fuller in flavor than the white.

VDN and VDL wines that have developed a rather pronounced oxidized flavor after long wood aging are granted a special AC: Rasteau VDN and VDL Rancio. Prolonged wood aging causes a wine to lose its freshness and fruit and become oxidized. In the case of Rasteau VDN and VDL Rancio wines, this oxidized aroma and flavor become more pronounced, and take on a definite rancid quality. This isn't as unappetizing as it may sound. But they say it is an acquired taste.

I have never come across *vin de liqueur* in any style, and suspect that although the AC is allowed, very little, if any, is now being made.

Normally the grapes for the unfortified Rasteau Côtes du Rhône Villages wines are harvested from September 20 to October 10. Those for the fortified *vin doux* are picked between October 10 and 20.

The Rasteau *vin doux* is usually the product of a single vintage, though it is not vintage-dated.

Rasteau *vin doux* requires maximum sunshine for the grapes to ripen sufficiently to achieve the high natural alcohol required for this wine. In years with little sun, very little *vin doux* is made. In 1975, 45,008 gallons (1,701 hectoliters) of white and 556 gallons (21 hectoliters) of red and rosé VDN were produced. The VDN production for 1974 totaled 61,784 gallons (2,335 hectoliters).

The maximum allowable yield of the grapes for the *vin doux* wines is 321 gallons/acre (30 hectoliters/hectare), although the INAO can raise or lower this maximum. If a vineyard gets a yield over 321 gallons/acre, the wine is normally déclassified. In some cases, though, special authorization is given by the INAO for the wine, but only after it has verified and approved the quality.

Most Rasteau wine—the fortified *vin doux naturel*, as well as the unfortified Côtes du Rhône Villages, and Côtes du Rhône table wine—is produced at the cooperative, Cave des Vignerons de Rasteau, which has approximately 120 members. In addition, some fifteen producers who don't belong to the co-op make their own wine. Some of those bottling a *vin doux naturel* are Emile Bressy (Domaine de la Grange Neuve), Maurice Charavin (Domaine du Charavin), Philippe Colombet, Julien Nicolet, and Francis Vache.

Charavin, one of the highly regarded independents, always produces his VDN from the grapes of a single harvest.

There's an interesting story behind this name, Charavin. At the time of the French Revolution, a stranger fleeing from the Reign of Terror was given refuge by a family in Rasteau. He worked in their vineyard in anonymity, revealing to no one who he was. Out of gratitude, he built a wine cart for the vigneron, and took his name from it—*char-a-vin*. To this day, the descendants who bear his name, Charavin, don't know what his real name was.

Generally the red *vin doux naturel* ferments in contact with the skins for two to three days to extract color. Both the red and the white VDN ferment for about six days at relatively warm temperatures before their spirits are lifted by the addition of brandy. The resultant VDN wine is aged for two to three years in oak (Russian and French) before being bottled.

Rasteau VDN, because of its high alcoholic and sugar content, will last quite well for two to three weeks after the bottle has been opened without deterioration.

Besides the fortified VDN and VDL, table wines also are produced in Rasteau. Rasteau is one of the villages allowed to use the Côtes du Rhône Villages AC. AC law sets a maximum yield of 375 gallons/acre (35 hectoliters/hectare) for the Côtes du Rhône Villages wine. In 1974, 58,212 gallons (2,200 hectoliters) of Villages wine was produced, and 74,432 gallons (2,813 hectoliters) in 1975. Also, much of the Rasteau table wine is bottled as a simple Côtes du Rhône. Under the Côtes du Rhône Villages AC, red, white, and rosé wines can be made. By far the largest portion of the Côtes du Rhône Villages wine is red. Next in importance, in terms of quantity, is the fortified *vin doux naturel*, followed by the rosé.

A minuscule amount of white table wine is produced from Grenache blanc, Clairette blanc, Ugni blanc, and Bourboulenc grapes. The rosé is the product of Grenache noir, Cinsault, and Carignane. The red is from a maximum of 65% Grenache noir and 10% Carignane, the remainder being Syrah and Mourvèdre. Many other varieties are allowed, according to the grapes specified for Côtes du Rhône Villages.

Besides meeting yield requirements, alcoholic requirements, aging requirements, and using the specified grape varieties, these wines must also meet taste requirements in order to rate the Côtes du Rhône Rasteau (Villages) AC.

The table wines of Côtes du Rhône Rasteau are best drunk within a few years of the vintage. It is claimed that the red will last and even improve with up to ten years of age. But I don't go along with this point of view. While there may be exceptions, the Rasteau reds that I have tasted didn't have sufficient tannin to last more than five or six years. Yet even if they had, since they are quite enjoyable in their third year already, why hold them until their tenth, or even their sixth? Wine, after all, is for enjoyment; and to enjoy it, you must drink it.

According to an old proud claim for the wine of Rasteau, "It has the goodness of Pope Boniface, the wit of good king René, the simplicity of Saint Francis, and the beauty of Queen Johanna."

13. BEAUMES DE VENISE

On the east bank of the Rhône river, in the department of Vaucluse, is Beaumes de Venise, a small wine village in the foothills of the Ventoux range. The village takes its name from a cave at the foot of a rocky crag and the name of the county, Comtat Venaissin (corrupted to Venise), in which it is located.

This quaint old village is full of history. A number of Gallo-Roman relics have been turned up in excavations here. There are churches dating from the eighth century, when the Saracens were finally expelled from Provence, and ruins of feudal castle as a reminder of those dark ages.

The history of the vine goes back a long way too. Pliny wrote in his *Natural History* that the Muscat had been cultivated for a long time in Balme (the Latin name for Beaumes).

According to local legend, Muscat vines were first planted in this area some 2,500 years ago by the Greeks of Marseille. The land here is well suited to the vine; the site is sunny and protected from the cold blast of the Mistral by the Dentelles de Montmirail to the north.

At the time of the seventh crusade, Louis IX (Saint Louis) came to this area with his queen, Marguerite de Provence. She, being a native of this region, introduced the king to the delights of the local Muscat wine.

On returning from the crusade the king is supposed to have given to the church at Beaumes a twig from the crown of thorns brought back from the Holy Land. Pilgrims who came to visit the shrine over the centuries (until the relic disappeared during the French Revolution) spread the fame of the Muscat of Beaumes.

This wine is believed to have been a favorite with the popes at Avignon, who had vines at Beaumes. Even after the papacy returned to Rome, the popes retained the vineyard in Beaumes.

In 1660 Louis XIV with the queen mother, Anne of Austria, and Cardinal Mazarin sojourned at Avignon. At the reception at the Palace of the Popes held in their honor the "Muscat of the Popes" was served.

This Muscat was said to be a very strong wine (perhaps a fortified wine then as it is today), and when the people drank too much they "went crazy." In the middle of the eighteenth century the excesses were such that Father Aquaviva, vice-legat in Avignon, decided to take drastic measures.

His measures went so far as to nearly forbid the drinking of Muscat altogether. It was forbidden to give something to eat or drink during the divine services and after eight P.M.; the sale of wine was forbidden to people who were suspected of eating and drinking too much. It was forbidden to swear, to curse, to sing, to play drums, to dance, to throw stones, or to fire guns—all things which had been common so far.

A stiff fine was imposed on any who broke the new laws, and men were hired to make sure that the laws were respected—well, if not respected, obeyed in any case.

The cultivation of the Muscat was stopped. The vineyards suffered, as did the vignerons, and the population of the Comtat Venaissin in general.

In 1766, Louis XV, dissatisfied with Pope Clement XIII's behavior (he allowed the Jesuits evicted from France to stay in the Comtat), annexed the Comtat Venaissin to France.

The people benefited from the new French laws. The restrictions on the Muscat disappeared, and the vineyards were brought to fruition once more.

Alas, joy was short. A few years later, in 1774, the Comtat was regained by the papacy and the old laws were applied again.

The Baron de Beaumes went to plead the cause of the Comtat and of its inhabitants before the apostolic chamber. The baron pleaded so well that the barony was raised to a dukedom. The Duke of Beaumes was beloved by his people, and suffered no harm during the French Revolution.

It must be said, though, that the Muscat production didn't flourish again for a long time after the harsh laws of Father Aquaviva. During the following two centuries the harvests were rather poor. In the beginning of the nineteenth century, olive trees and wheat were the major crops in this area, and only a nominal amount of Muscat was grown in Beaumes de Venise.

Then, when phylloxera devastated the vineyards, it seemed that the long history of the Muscat of Beaumes de Venise had come to an end. Abbot Allègre, writing at the end of the nineteenth century, lamented, "The Muscat vines are dead and of the famous Muscat only the memory is left."

But the twentieth century has seen a turnabout, and the Muscat of Beaumes de Venise is again gaining favor.

Beaumes de Venise produces one of the two *vins doux naturels* (VDNs) of the Côtes du Rhône granted the protection of the AC laws. The other VDN with an AC is that of Rasteau to the north.

The *vin doux naturel* of Beaumes de Venise is the product of *Muscat à petits grains ronds* (the Muscat of the little round berries). The vines are planted on terraced slopes in soft, sandy soil with admixtures of chalk and clay. The vines for the VDN are planted on approximately 457 acres (185 hectares), mostly in Beaumes de Venise. A small portion is in part of the village of Aubignan.

Records indicate that at one time Muscat vines were trained horizontally on the terraces, with the vines stretching along the ground instead of upward, so that the grapes, catching the extra sunlight reflected from the retaining walls, would ripen more fully and become sweeter. Supposedly there are still some vines planted in this fashion in the remote places in the hills, but these vines are quite old. Vines planted more recently—which is most of them—are trained in the normal upright fashion.

As with the VDN of Rasteau, the *vin doux naturel* of Beaumes de Venise is never vintage-dated. It is presumably the product of a single year, at least in most vintages, but in poor years some wine from the previous vintage will be blended in.

Beaumes de Venise is known for its sweet, fortified Muscat, but red, white, and rosé table wines are also made here. Most of the VDN, and most of the other wines of Beaumes de Venise, are produced at a large cooperative. This modern co-op, founded in 1956, looks rather like a factory with its large stainless steel and enamel tanks, its pipes and valves.

Some 320 growers belong to the co-op, which produces about 80% of the Beaumes de Venise *vins doux naturel*. Two major shippers who bottle a VDN are Paul Jaboulet and J. Vidal Fleury. Other *vins doux*, bottled under the name of the estate (*domaine*) producing them, are Domaine Durban and Domaine Les Bernadins (L. Castaud) in Beaumes de Venise, and Domaine St.-Sauveur in Aubignan.

From the small vintage of 1975, 87,159 gallons (3,294 hectoliters) of VDN were produced; the total output of the prolific 1974 vintage was 135,290 gallons (5,113 hectoliters). Neither vintage achieved the maximum allowable yield of 300 gallons/acre (28 hectoliters/hectare) although 1974 came close.

The co-op has a storage capacity of 1,587,600 gallons (60,000 hectoliters) and an average annual production of 793,800 to 926,100 gallons (30,000 to 35,000 hectoliters). Of this total, 317,520 to 476,280 gallons (12,000 to 18,000 hectoliters) are Beaumes de Venise red (a Côtes du Rhône AC wine), 158,760 to 211,680 gallons (6,000 to 8,000 hectoliters) Côtes du Ventoux red, and 52,920 to 105,840 gallons (2,000 to 4,000 hectoliters) Muscat VDN. The remainder is *vin du pays*, little of which is sold in bottle.

Beaumes de Venise red, a vintage-dated Côtes du Rhône wine, is a blend of 80% Grenache with Cinsault, Carignan, Syrah, and Mourvèdre making up the rest. This wine, like most regional Côtes du Rhônes, is best when young, while it is still fresh and fruity.

The Côtes du Ventoux comes from some sixty villages in the area around Mount Ventoux, southwest of Orange. These wines—red, white and rosé—range in quality from ordinary to fair, and should be consumed in their youth; there is nothing to be gained by aging them.

The Muscat Beaumes de Venise *vin doux naturel*, too, is best drunk while it is still young and fresh. It goes well with fresh fruit, especially melon.

14. LIRAC

Viniculture and viticulture in Lirac may go back to when this was a Roman province. At castle de Clary, a well-known estate in this region, were found the remains of a Roman farm with vats for fermenting wine. So it is believed that the Romans were making wine here centuries ago.

Some of the estates in Lirac have interesting histories. Wine making at Château St.-Roch goes back to at least the fifteenth century. The period from 1475 to 1600 was quite a prosperous one for this estate.

During the phylloxera scourge in the last century vineyards were uprooted and the vines replaced by olive trees. It took approximately three-quarters of a century for wine production in Lirac to regain its pre-phylloxera status.

The vineyards in Lirac, today, are much larger than they were before phylloxera. Before the invasion of this root louse, the vineyards of Lirac were relatively small.

It was not until 1947 that the French government granted AC status to the red, white, and rosé wines of Lirac.

Lirac, like its better known neighbor to the south, Tavel, is known for its rosé wine. But Lirac red is increasing in importance and today rivals the rosé. Some fifteen to twenty years ago Lirac produced mostly rosé, and that continued to be the case up until four years ago. Now it makes more red wine. Interestingly enough, once the growers began to get involved with the red wine, seven or eight years ago, it was only a few years before red wine production began to surpass that of the rosé.

Lirac is allowed to produce red, white, and rosé wine, an unusual situation in the Côtes du Rhône. Except for the regional Côtes du Rhône and the somewhat more specific Côtes du Rhône Villages, no AC in the Côtes du Rhône region allows all three types of table wine. And, outside Lirac, the only local (as opposed to regional) ACs in the Côtes du Rhône which allow a rosé table wine are Gigondas and Tavel. A few of the estates in Lirac produce all three wines, but most make only two.

The Lirac AC covers the wines of four villages: Lirac, Roquemaure, St.-Geniés-de-Comolas, and St.-Laurent-des-Arbres. The vineyards of these four villages cover 1,722 acres (697 hectares). One-third of the acreage is in Roquemaure; the remainder is divided among the others.

Lirac itself is a sleepy little village of only about 250 inhabitants. Around the village you see fields of grain and orchards as well as the vineyards. Here and there are pine trees, and cypress trees lined up in dark green rows as windbreaks protecting the vines against the Mistral. Within the vineyards only olive and mulberry trees are allowed. It is, however, forbidden to plant trees in the new vineyards. And, by law, time is running out for the trees in the older vineyards; shortly they have to be uprooted.

Roquemaure, the largest of the four towns under the Lirac AC is, reputedly, where Hannibal with his legions and his pachyderm parade crossed the Rhône on their way to Italy over the Alps. This village is west and slightly north of Lirac, and not far from Châteauneuf-du-Pape to the north and east. A small part of Roquemaure is entitled to use the Tavel AC for its rosé.

St.-Laurent-des-Arbres, surrounded by the ramparts of old

fortifications, lies north and slightly to the east of Lirac. St.-Geniés-de-Comolas, another of the wine towns, is north and slightly east of St.-Laurent.

To qualify for AC Lirac, the wine must be tasted and approved by an official panel of tasters.

AC laws require that the vines of Lirac be planted on slopes or hilly countryside. Sometimes there are vineless patches between vineyards. If INAO officials do not consider the land high or dry enough, any vines planted there may not be used for AC Lirac wines. Those planted on the flatlands can be used only for Côtes du Rhône regionals or *vins du pays*.

The soil here is clay and chalk with some sand. It tends to be a mix of two types of soil together. In some parts there is also red gravel and stone. The viticulturist of Lirac demonstrates his knowledge and ability in matching the different vines to the different soils, not always an easy task.

As elsewhere in the southern Côtes du Rhône, many varieties of vines are allowed. The red and rosé must contain at least 40% Grenache, which in combination with Cinsault and Mourvèdre must make up no less than 60% of the total. Other varieties that are allowed are Syrah, Bourboulenc, Calitor, Picpoul, Clairette, Ugni blanc, Maccabéo, and up to 10% Carignan. The Clairette, Ugni blanc, and Maccabéo, though, are not much used.

White Lirac must be made from at least 33% Clairette and with no more than 25% of any one of the following: Bourboulenc, Calitor, Grenache, Maccabéo, Picpoul, Ugni blanc. Clairette and Bourboulenc are the white varieties most commonly used here.

For all these varieties, the minimum and maximum percentages refer to the amount planted in the vineyard and not the amount used in the wine. This latter amount might vary from year to year depending on the weather—not all varieties ripen together. As an example, Château St.-Roch, one or Lirac's most important estates, has the following varieties planted in its 91-acre (37-hectare) vineyard: Grenache (41%), Cinsault (24%), Mourvèdre (14%), Syrah (12%), Bourboulenc (4%), Carignan (3%), and Clairette (2%).

The vines themselves (the bearing portion, not the rootstock) must be at least four years old to be used for the AC wine.

In addition to these regulations, the laws of controlled appellation also set down rules governing irrigation. It is forbidden except in the case of a severe drought, when one of several waterings are permitted. These waterings must not be so heavy that the vineyards are submerged. Submersion is strictly forbidden. Some growers in Lirac say that the regulation doesn't specify who is to decide when the drought is severe enough. To date no irrigation has been authorized.

AC specifies that the maximum yield cannot exceed 375 gallons/acre (35 hectoliters/hectare). Judging by the production in 1974 and 1975, it isn't much of a problem to stay below the maximum: 1975—red and rosé, 280,820 gallons (10,613 hectoliters), white, 2,408 gallons (91 hectoliters); 1974—red and rosé, 307,809 gallons (11,633 hectoliters), white, 2,408 gallons (91 hectoliters).

The *Ban de Vendange* (announcement setting the date of the harvest) is published by a commission that decides when the grapes are ready for picking.

As a rule of thumb, red Lirac is fermented in contact with the skins for five to seven days. Some of the stems are kept in the fermentation vats, as well, to extract even more tannin.

The wine is generally aged for one year in small casks or large vats before being bottled. AC specifies that the red cannot leave the estate before the May 1 following the harvest, but in fact most of it is still in cooperage at that point. Russian oak cooperage, as in other areas of the southern Côtes du Rhône, is common. Austrian oak and chestnut are also used.

Lirac rosé achieves its color by "bleeding"—the white juice picks up its pink color from being in contact with the skins for about fifteen hours.

The rosé and the white are generally kept in stainless steel or enamel tanks to preserve their freshness. While some estates still age the rosé in wood, this is more the exception than the rule.

Generally the rosé and white are offered on the market shortly after the bottling, whereas the red might not be released for up to four years. The estates try to hold the red until it is drinkable, not necessarily at its best. In fact, Lirac red generally reaches its peak from six to eight years, but should last for a decade.

Both the rosé and the white should be consumed while they still retain their youthful freshness and fruitiness.

The white has a pronounced grapiness on the nose and in the mouth. The rosé, like that of Tavel, is quite full and dry with a pronounced fruitiness. The red has a spicy fragrance. It is full-bodied with lots of fruit and a firm texture. Red Lirac is a good choice to drink with roast meats, steaks, and chops. The white goes well with fish; the rosé with pork or poultry.

A local cooperative, SICA Les Producteurs de Lirac, with 180 members bottles much of the production of these wines. Other important growers: J. Assemat (Domaine Les Garriques); Marcel Beaumont; Degoul (Château de Bouchassy); Domaines Cantegril-Le Sablon; Domaine des Causses et St.-Eynes; Domaine J. Duseigneur; Domaine Rousseau; Domaine Sabon; Fuget (Château de Boucarut); Granier (Domaine de la Croze); Leperchois (Les Carabiniers); J & M Lombardo (Domaine du Devoy); Marius Mayer (Domaine de Clary); Joseph Pelaquie; Pons-Mure (Domaine La Tour de Lirac); Mme. Marie Pons-Mure (Domaine de Castel-Oualou); Henri de Regis (Château Ségriès); ' A. Verda (Château St.-Roch); Roussel (Domaine de la Charetière).

As a rule of thumb, out of ten vintages one is exceptional, two are good, four are average, two are fair, and one poor. The vintages are more important for the red wine than for the rosé or the white. This is because the weather is less of a factor for these wines.

The grapes for the red wine need a year with enough sunshine to ripen fully and achieve good color as well as sufficient sugar to meet the minimum alcohol required. The grapes for the rosé and the white wines need fewer sunny days as they are more desirable with higher levels of acidity and lower alcohol than the red. The rosé and white wines, further, are served chilled, which tends to cut down on their acid to the taste.

And, of the white, so little is produced that the vintner can pick and choose among the grapes in most years to produce a good wine. Most of the grapes grown in Lirac are used to produce red and rosé wines.

Recent vintages: 1975—good to very good; 1974—good to average; 1973—average to good; 1972—mediocre to average; 1971—good to average; 1970—exceptional; 1969—much of the crop was destroyed by hailstorms; 1968—very uneven, some good, some not; 1967—an exceptional vintage; 1966—uneven; 1965—middling; 1963—the worst since World War II.

15. TAVEL

The vineyards of Tavel, 8 miles west of Avignon, lie in the midst of olive groves and apricot trees. These vineyards are famous for producing the best rosé of France.

Tavel rosé has been famous since the seventeenth century, but it was known and appreciated long before. Philippe le Bel, king of France in the thirteenth century, gave it the royal nod, declaring that there is no good wine outside Tavel. Its renown was boosted again when the popes, in the fourteenth century, drank the rosé of Tavel. They enjoyed it well enough to ask that some be sent to Rome. Cardinal Richelieu also mentions Tavel rosé early in the seventeenth century. The French poet Ronsard called Tavel "sunshine in flagons." Louis XIV, Balzac, Daudet, and the great gastronome Brillat-Savarin are among some of the other luminaries who have drunk and enjoyed Tavel rosé.

As in other areas of the Côtes du Rhône, Roman ruins have been found here too. Consequently speculation has it that the Romans made wine here, but no Roman winemaking utensils have been found.

This small hillside village of fewer than a thousand inhabitants dates from the Roman period. The village takes its name from Tavellis, the Latin name for this area. This was later shortened to Tavels, then Tavel, as it is known today. Six miles from town is a river with the same root name, La Tave.

Some of the houses in Tavel incorporate the remains of buildings dating from the eighth century. And the oldest reference to Tavel rosé dates from the ninth century. In a letter to Bishop Tructarias of Bézières dated July 16, 897, Viscount Rainard mentions the rosé of Tavel. And it's not surprising that the subject should have come up, as Rainard had obtained the village of Tavel from that same Bishop Tructarias.

One of the oldest vineyards of Tavel, the Prieuré de Montézarques, was known in the fourteenth century. It is one of the most important Tavel vineyards today. There were five castles in Tavel in the fourteenth century. Montézarques was one; the others were Château de Clary, Domaine de Trinquevedel, Domaine de Manissy, and Château d'Aqueria. These others are also important vineyards today.

Charles Odoyer, a local historian and proprietor of Clos du Palais, says that this neighborhood of Tavel where his winery is located is called Palais because at one time there was a palace here.

Before phylloxera there was a small vineyard in this neighborhood, where now there are houses. Perhaps the two huge, over-100-year-old Jacquez vines growing over the winery door and along the side of the building are the only vines left here now.

M. Odoyer, a retired schoolmaster, makes his wines in the old cellar—which used to be a stable for donkeys, horses, and sheep—under his eighteenth-century house. This tiny cellar, he says, is typical of the old Tavel cellars.

The Tavel rosé of Clos du Palais is the *best* that I've tasted.

Wine has been made in Tavel since the eighth century except for a short period after phylloxera. Tavel was one of the earliest areas struck by phylloxera, in 1867. Shortly after this root louse devastated some of the vineyards hereabouts the vines were uprooted and were not replanted until 1885, when replanting on grafted roots began. Today all the vines are grafted onto American rootstock.

The vineyards near Arles were flooded for forty days and forty nights in an attempt to drown 'em (the phylloxera) right out. The flooding granted the farmers a temporary reprieve. But not for long. The pest soon began to munch away at the roots again, and have a feast of a time.

In Tavel the land wasn't flat enough to attempt flooding. The soil of Tavel is sandy and phylloxera doesn't thrive in sand as it does in other types of soil. In the sandier places some of the vines survived. But partly from fear of this pest, and partly from disgust the vines were uprooted.

Olive trees were planted in place of the ripped-out vines, the olive being another plant that does well in poor soil. Attempts were made to grow wheat, even to raise chickens and rabbits, "anything to stay alive." Between 1900 and 1902 much of the population, especially young people, left Tavel for jobs in factories and on the railroads. Often, small family-owned vineyards were maintained by part of the family while the rest left to find work in the cities. They sent home money to replant the vineyards with grafted vines. They began to return after World War I as a postwar recession had led to a collapse in industry and many factories closed.

In 1922, 79,380 gallons (3,000 hectoliters) of Tavel were produced; today it's 529,200-793,800 gallons (20-30,000 hectoliters). In 1975 Tavel produced 528,433 gallons (19,971 hectoliters) of wine; in 1974, 761,307 gallons (28,722 hectoliters).

The vineyards of Tavel cover 1,779 acres (720 hectares),

part of which are in neighboring Roquemaure. Most of the vines in Roquemaure, though, are covered by AC Lirac. New plantings are replacing forestlands.

Tavel is separated from Lirac by a stretch of land 1¼-2 miles (2-3 kilometers) long and 656-984 feet (200-300 meters) wide. When the ACs were granted, this land was covered by a forest. When the trees were cut down, about ten years ago, vines were planted there. It is not Tavel, not Lirac. The vines there are covered under the Côtes du Rhône AC.

Château d'Aqueria is at the beginning of Tavel, on the line dividing Tavel from this no-man's land.

Up until World War II other crops were planted along with the vines. Since the war promiscuous cultivation has been abandoned. Today vines are replacing other crops.

Nowadays Tavel is shipped in bottle—the clear Rhine-style bottle; but before World War I it was sent in barrel to shippers who bottled it and labeled it Tavel Rosé.

Another practice that has changed in Tavel is the method of pressing. Just prior to World War I the first wine presses arrived in Tavel. Until that time foot power was used. M. Odoyer of Clos du Palais still uses a small basket press.

Tavel rosé is the product of at least two, and as many as nine grape varieties, none of which may exceed 60%: Grenache, Cinsault (minimum 15%), Carignane (maximum 10%), Clairette, Picpoul, Bourboulenc, Mourvèdre, Syrah, and Calitor. This last variety is rarely used today and is gradually being replaced. If more than 30% Calitor is used and the wine is declassified, the Côtes du Rhône AC cannot be used.

The vineyards of Clos du Palais are in five separate parcels scattered throughout Tavel. Grenache dominates, but there are also Cinsault, Bourboulenc, Clairette, Carignane, and

Picpoul varieties. M. Odoyer says that before phylloxera all the Tavel vineyards were very, very small, but they each had all the grape varieties for the blend.

The maximum allowable yield by law is 450 gallons/acre (42 hectoliters/hectare); if a vineyard produces over 514 gallons/acre (48 hectoliters/hectare), the entire crop is declassified.

Jacquez, a vine grown commonly here years ago, has since fallen out of favor, to be replaced by Grenache. It was just a mediocre to ordinary grape, but it was resistant to phylloxera. It is a rather dubious reflection on the quality of the wine it produced that it wasn't planted in place of grafted vines against the devastation of phylloxera. It sometimes is used in the Côtes du Rhône as rootstock though, but because of its resistance to a certain fungus, not to phylloxera.

The vines are planted on slopes and in the valleys of La Cèze on the plains of Gard. The soil on the slopes is mostly pebbles and clay while that in the valley is mostly sand with some outcroppings of flintstone and calcium. Most of the growers own plots both on the slopes and in the valley and they make no distinction between valley and hillside grapes, blending them all together. Originally vines were planted only on the slopes.

In the old days the village elders made the decision when the harvest would begin. Early picking was firmly discouraged. The seigneur of Tavel, however, was granted a grace period—a three-day headstart. Maybe he was a very slow picker.

From the beginning Tavel was known for its rosé wine. How rosé wine first came to be made here is only conjecture. It is supposed that an attempt was made to produce a white wine from red grapes and the juice wasn't separated from the skins soon enough. Quite naturally, this resulted in a pink wine.

Today, depending on the temperature, Tavel rosé is fermented in contact with the skins from six to twenty-four hours to extract the desired color.

Clos du Palais, a minuscule estate with an average annual production of 275 cases or 661.5 gallons (25 hectoliters), and Château d'Aqueria, a large estate of 111 acres (45 hectares) with an annual production of about 42,335 gallons (1,600 hectoliters), both use traditional methods in producing their wines. The wine is fermented and aged in wood. Most other wineries in Tavel now ferment and age the wines in stainless steel vats. It is becoming more and more difficult, and more and more expensive to use wood cooperage. The skilled coopers who make and repair the wooden casks and vats are becoming a thing of the past. The oak used at Tavel is mainly from Russia and Scandinavia. M. Odoyer ferments in a 317.5 gallon (12 hectoliter) open oak cask.

Tavel, usually bottled when it is a year old, is at its best at two years of age. It will last for about five or six years. Reputedly Tavel rosé ages very well, but I've never come across a good one over six years old.

At one time a wine was made in Tavel for home consumption that they called "Piquette." It was actually made by adding water to the lees left from making the regular wine. It is rarely, if ever, done anymore, but the word "Piquette" is still used to mean poor wine.

Tavel rosé is a full-bodied, sturdy wine with a firm backbone and an attractive dry fruitiness. Its bouquet hints of apricots. It is a good choice to accompany pork, especially roast pork, and ham. Some noted authorities recommend Tavel rosé with oysters because of its dryness, but I'll stick with Chablis with my oysters, or as an acceptable alternative, Muscadet.

M. de Bez of Château d'Aqueria serves his rosé with apricots grown in part of his vineyards, and the wine goes surprisingly well.

Hostellerie du Seigneur, in the village of Tavel, offers a fine selection of local wines and dishes. It is a good place to enjoy duck with olives. The food is first class.

In 1935 a cooperative of growers was formed; in 1938 the co-op opened. Today most of the 170-plus growers belong to this cooperative, which bottles about half of the wines of Tavel.

Important estates and growers include, besides Clos du Palais and Château d'Aqueria, Domaine de Montézarques, Domaine de Trinquevedel, Cru du Vieux Moulin de Tavel, Clos de Vaucroze, Christian Amido, Domaine de la Genestière, Domaine de Lonval, Domaine de Manissy, Marcel Fraissinet, Raoul de Lanzac, Gabriel Leveque, Domaine de la Forcadière (Armand Maby, Mayor of Tavel), and Clos Canto-Perdrix.

The vintners of Tavel point out that the differences in a wine are less noticeable from year to year in a rosé than in a red. And besides, they add, the sun always shines in Tavel.

Rosé owes more to the soil and grape varieties than to the weather. The skill of the grower is, of course, crucially important. He mustn't pick too late in hot years or too soon in cooler ones. The alcohol and acidity balance will vary from year to year, but not by much. Cooler years will be higher in acidity and lower in alcohol; the reverse is true for warmer years.

AC requires at least 11% alcohol; 12.5% is more normal.

Evaluation of recent vintages: 1975—average to good;

1974—better than '75; 1973—average, somewhat light; 1972—
mediocre, perhaps the weather was too hot; 1971—average;
1970—varied, some average wines, some exceptional; 1969—
exceptional; 1968—very poor; 1967—exceptional; 1965, 1963—
very poor, among the worst ever.

16. GIGONDAS

On the east bank of the Rhône river in the department of Vaucluse lies the small wine village of Gigondas with approximately 700 inhabitants. Above this village rise the Dentelles de Montmirail, named for their slender needles and "lacy" crests of Jurassic limestone.

There seems to be some uncertainty over the origins of the name Gigondas. Some scholars believe that Gigondas is a corruption of the Latin name *Jucundum*, meaning joyful country. Another theory has it that the name is a derivative of *Jiguit Undas*, country of water, or where water springs from the earth. This seems the more likely, for not only is that name more similar, but there are a number of springs in this area.

Gigondas lies east and north of Orange, north and slightly west of Carpentras, south and somewhat west of Vaison-la-Romaine, putting it almost in the center of a triangle with Roman cities at each apex.

Gigondas is on one of the Roman routes. A road was built along the side of the mountain here by the Romans, who often built roads in the provinces on the hillsides rather than in the valleys, for strategic reasons.

Where the Roman legions went, the vine was often planted, to provide the soldiers with a wholesome beverage. Many Roman ruins have been found in this area, some containing utensils used in winemaking and wine drinking. To further the view that the Romans made wine here, there is mention in the writings of Pliny of the wines of Gigondas.

With this long history of winemaking it seems strange that the reputation of Gigondas wine is quite young, dating from only about 1930. Although Gigondas was not well known, the vintages of 1925 and 1929 were highly regarded and justifiably, I'm told, quite famous.

The newness of Gigondas's reputation as a wine region might be due to the fact that its olive crop was much more important up until 1929. Besides having an exceptionally fine vintage that year, a frost killed most of the olive trees, thereby increasing the importance of the vine. There are still some olive trees growing here, their silvery gray leaves rising above the rows of vines in some vineyards. There are also apricot trees, which do well in the same dry conditions and help to protect the vines from the blast of the Mistral.

Gigondas today has only two industries: viticulture and viniculture. In fact, the grape grows profusely here covering nearly 2,470 acres (1,000 hectares).

Until 1971 Gigondas was entitled to use only the AC Côtes du Rhône Villages. Since then, Gigondas has been awarded its own AC for red and rosé wines.

Wine has been made in Gigondas from those early days, continuously, except for a few years after phylloxera struck the vineyards. During the phylloxera crisis the devastated vineyards were abandoned. For about ten years, from 1880 to 1890, the garance plant was cultivated here. This plant was used for making a dye for cloth, especially for the trousers of the nineteenth-century French army uniform.

It used to be that Gigondas was known for its rosé, but today its reputation is based on a red wine that is similar, in some respects, to Châteauneuf-du-Pape. Gigondas is generally, though, deeper in color and slower-maturing than Châteauneuf-du-Pape.

Since World War II the red wines of Gigondas have been increasing in popularity. Forty-five years ago, 60% of the wines of Gigondas were rosé. Today less than 20% is rosé and this is decreasing. Thirty years ago an old Gigondas rosé was the preferred wine here.

Gigondas red, which now accounts for over 70% of the wine of this village, is the product of 65% (maximum) Grenache noir and at least 25% Syrah, with the addition of Mourvèdre, Cinsault, and up to 10% of the other varieties allowed in AC Côtes du Rhône except for Carignane. Some vineyards, I've been told, grow only Syrah and Mourvèdre.

The Syrah is planted on the upper slopes, in soil of chalk and stone, at altitudes of up to 1,641 feet (500 meters). This variety is an early ripener. Plantings of the Syrah are increasing at the expense of Grenache.

Vines are planted on both the slopes and the flats here, with vineyards on the hillsides more common.

The soil of Gigondas is made up of clay, limestone, pebbles, and rocks with some prehistoric flintstone.

Gigondas rosé, which along with the red is entitled to use the Gigondas AC, is the product of up to 60% Grenache noir, at least 15% Cinsault, and up to 25% of the other allowable Côtes du Rhône varieties except Carignane. As with the red, Mourvèdre is commonly used in the rosé.

Gigondas rosé achieves its color by "bleeding," as do Tavel and Lirac wines. The must is left in contact with the skins just long enough for the juice to pick up sufficient color—from two hours to two days.

Gigondas white, which amounts to less than 10% of the output of this village, is entitled to use only the regional Côtes du Rhône appellation. This wine is the product of Grenache blanc and Clairette blanc in nearly even amounts.

Trellis pruning is allowed, but only one wire can be used

for training the vines. This type of pruning is becoming more common, as it is easier to work with.

Gigondas AC allows the vineyards two waterings per year if done prior to July 14, none afterward. Reportedly, though, no one has ever taken advantage of this regulation in Gigondas. They have so far gotten by with the natural rainfall.

The harvest here normally takes place from the end of October through the middle of November. As in Château-neuf-du-Pape, AC law requires that part of the crop be discarded. That portion of grapes that is rejected after selecting the best grapes is called the *rapé*. The minimum amount of *rapé* is 5%, but in some vintages 10% or even 15% of the harvest is rejected.

Generally, Gigondas red is fermented in contact with the skins for about ten days, but rarely, if ever, over twelve days. The stalks are also included in the fermenting must in order to extract more tannin. Following fermentation, the wine is put into 926-2,117-gallon (35-80-hectoliter) oak, generally Russian oak, casks for approximately two years.

Appellation requires a 12.5% alcoholic minimum, but 14% is more common for the red. This is the highest alcoholic minimum in France; it is equaled by a few other appellations but not surpassed for a table wine. The maximum yield is 375 gallons/acre (35 hectoliters/hectare) excluding the *rapé*. The average yield in Gigondas is from 268-321 gallons/acre (25-30 hectoliters/hectare). If the yield exceeds 428 gallons/acre (40 hectoliters/hectare), the entire vineyard loses the right to the AC and is declassified.

In 1975, a small vintage, some 463,129 gallons (17,503 hectoliters) of AC Gigondas (red and rosé) was produced. The previous vintage amounted to a total of 707,884 gallons (26,753 hectoliters).

This production comes from approximately 2,446 acres (990 hectares) of vines. Pierre Amadieu, the largest grower, owns 247 acres (100 hectares).

About 120 growers, of the approximately 150 in Gigondas, belong to the local cooperative cellar. This co-op produces about one-third of the total output here. The member growers are under no obligation to give a minimum to the co-op. In fact, they need not give any of their crop to the cooperative if they choose not to. Wines from the co-op are labeled Caves des Vignerons. The red wine is labeled Gigondas Baumanière.

Two other notable producers are François Ay (Château Raspail) and Hilarion Roux & Fils (Les Pallières). The cellars of Les Pallières, built into the hill, are among the oldest in Gigondas, dating back some 250 years. The vineyards cover approximately 662 acres (25 hectares). Some 25 to 30% of their production is rosé, and aside from a minuscule amount of white, the remainder is red.

Other notable grower-producers: Jean et Maurice Archimboud (Domaine de Montmirail), Henri Borruol (Domaine de St.-Cosme), Pierre Bezert, Raymond Boutiere (Domaine du Pesquier), Roger Chapalain (Domaine de Longue Toque), Edmond Chauvet (Domaine le Peage), Paul Chauvet (Le Grapillon d'Or), Roger Combe & Fils (Domaine de la Fourmone), M. Coulouvrat (Domaine Ste.-Anne), Georges Faraud, André Gras (Domaine St.-François-Xavier), Gabriel Meffre (Domaine des Bosquets), Roger Meffre (Domaine St.-Gayan), Laurent Meunier (La Gardette), Pierre Quiot (Les Pradets), Georges Richard (La Baumette), Charles Roux (Château du Trignon), and Pierre Veyrat (Château St.-André).

Of the recent vintages, 1975 and 1974 were good. The 1973 was uneven—the grapes harvested from the hillsides were good, but those from the valleys were, at best, only average. The 1972 reds will be long-lived, The 1971s and 1970s were good but less so than the very good 1969s. The poor years were 1968, 1965, and 1963. The best vintage of the past decade was 1967, which was exceptional. The more highly regarded 1966 vintage, while good, was not as good. The 1959 vintage was perhaps the best vintage since World War II.

Gigondas red is, generally, a deep-colored, ruby red wine with a rich, spicy aroma with overtones of black pepper—a frequent characteristic in Côtes du Rhône wines. This robust, full-bodied wine has a lot of fruit and tannin and generally will require four to eight years to develop. The better ones will last even longer.

Gigondas red is a good wine with braised beef, pot roast, or more robust meats such as venison.

A good place to enjoy the local wine in Gigondas is the Hostellerie Les Florets up on the hillside. As you sip your Gigondas and sample the regional specialties, you can look out over a view of the scenic countryside highlighted by the Dentelles de Montmirail, especially nice if you have a table under the trees.

17. CHATEAUNEUF-DU-PAPE

Châteauneuf-du-Pape, halfway between Avignon and Orange, on the left bank of the Rhône, lies at the center of the largest concentration of vineyards in the Côtes du Rhône. The history of Châteauneuf-du-Pape is closely linked to Avignon, ten miles to the southwest. The wines of Châteauneuf came into prominence during the "Babylonian captivity" (1309-1378) when the popes were at Avignon.

Though there is some speculation that the Romans may have made wine at Châteauneuf, there is no proof and very little that could be offered as evidence. Roman artifacts—coins, tiles, and pottery—have been found in this area. At nearby Orange there are the well-preserved theater and triumphal arch, splendid reminders of its days as a Roman colony. Numerous temples, amphitheaters, aqueducts, and other impressive ruins from Roman times dot the landscape throughout the southern Côtes du Rhône. There is no doubt that the Romans were here—and no doubt drinking wine—but whether the wine was also being made here is an unanswered question. Not much, if anything, in the way of Roman winemaking utensils has been found in the vicinity of Châteauneuf-du-Pape.

The old story about the Roman wine amphorae is a charming legend nonetheless. It seems that some Roman amphorae were unearthed in the village of Châteauneuf. And when they were examined—*voilà*—there was still some fine old Châteauneuf-du-Pape wine in them!

Some writers say that Hannibal passed through this area in 218 BC at the head of 60,000 men, on his route to Rome over the Alps. But no traces have been found here of that magnificent parade.

The written history of Châteauneuf begins on May 16, 908, when Louis l'Aveugle, the son of Bozon, king of Burgundy and Provence, gave the territory between Sorgues and the Rhône, including Bédarrides and the village now known as Châteauneuf-du-Pape, to the bishop of Avignon. Châteauneuf was to remain the property of the church up until the French Revolution.

In 1157, Frederick Barbarossa confirmed the donation of lands with a charter in which the name Châteauneuf (or *castrum novum*—documents being written in Latin in those days) appeared for the first time. Why it was called the "new castle" is something of a mystery, as no old castle is known to have been there before.

Toward the end of the twelfth century, the Knights Templar were established at Châteauneuf. They fortified the château, built a church, and planted vines. This vineyard is still there below the ruins of the château.

The link between Châteauneuf and the popes was established at the time of the Albigensian crusade. The Albigensian crusade pitted the church of Rome against the Albigenses, a heretical sect. The Albigenses, who defied the authority of the church, attracted considerable support among the nobility of southern France, who resented church interference in their affairs.

Much of Provence was destroyed when Louis VIII descended with his army on the Valley of the Rhône in 1226 to wage a vicious war—perhaps massacre is a more accurate word—against them, and to win back Avignon for the bishops. In 1229, the treaty marking the end of the crusade gave the papacy, from the spoils of war, the Comtat Venaissin. This would link the fate of the papacy with Avignon and Châteauneuf.

By the turn of the century, the church had become very powerful, and the popes meddled in the internal affairs of the European states. Philippe le Bel, the strong-willed French monarch, resisted this interference with his powers. In his dispute with Pope Boniface VIII, he had Boniface thrown into prison. There he was mistreated to force his compliance and not released until he consented to Philippe's demands. Shortly afterward, he died, possibly from the treatment he had suffered at the hands of his captors. He was succeeded briefly by Pope Benoît, who died in 1304.

Philippe le Bel decided to see to it that the next pope would be subservient to his will. He was powerful enough to influence the French cardinals to vote as he wished. In 1305, after an eleven-month deadlock, the College of Cardinals elected Bertrand de Got, the archbishop of Bordeaux, the new pope.

His election was unusual for two reasons (not counting the behind-the-scenes manipulation): De Got was not a cardinal, he was only a bishop, and he was not an Italian bishop, but a French one.

De Got, who took the name of Clement V, is credited with planting vines in Bordeaux, and is the pope for whom Château Pape Clément, in Graves, is named. But Clement seems to have done little for viticulture in the Côtes du Rhône. He did, however, move the papal seat to France—to the Comtat Venaissin—in 1309, and thus began the second "Babylonian captivity."

The meaning of this expression, Babylonian captivity, in reference to the popes at Avignon, was the submission of spiritual authority to secular domination. For it appeared to many observers, and not without reason, that the popes in France took their direction from the kings of France.

Pope John XXII (1318-1334), successor to Clement V, is credited with extending the vineyards and bringing importance to the wines of Châteauneuf. He also restored and enlarged the castle there, using it for his summer residence.

The Knights Templar were no longer there. Philippe le Bel had ordered their imprisonment, confiscating their considerable wealth. Pope Clement, at Philippe's bidding, suppressed the order, which soon died out.

At about this time, Châteauneuf acquired the surname Calcernier for the many lime kilns in the vicinity, perhaps kept especially active by the restoration work on the château. In a document dated 1584, the village was referred to as "Châteauneuf Calcernier called du Pape."

Benedict XII (1334-1342) began construction on the Palace of the Popes in Avignon. His successor, Clement VI (1342-1353), purchased the city of Avignon in 1348 from Countess Jeanne of Provence. It was to remain the property of the popes until, during the French Revolution, in 1791, when it was reunited with France.

Pope Clement VI had a splendid court which attracted artists and scholars, both at Avignon and Châteauneuf-du-Pape. During his years the village of Châteauneuf grew in size, and the vineyards were extended.

We don't know just when the first Châteauneuf-du-Pape wine was drunk by the popes. But in the accounts of the Apostolic Chambers it is noted that, in 1360, Innocent VI requested the white wine of Châteauneuf, and again, in 1361, the pope called for the red Châteauneuf wine from the papal cellar.

It is believed that Innocent VI (1353-1362) would have returned the papal seat to Rome if his poor health hadn't prevented him. Urban V (1362-1370), the monk pope, left Avignon to go to Rome in 1367. He stayed there for two years, but returned to Avignon, where he died shortly afterward. His successor, Gregory XI (1371-1377), was the last pope in Avignon.

Gregory made a brief visit to Rome in 1377 and died there. Under the threat of violence from Roman mobs, the Italian cardinals elected an Italian pope, Urban VI, who resided in Rome. In France, Clement VII was elected pope, and remained in Avignon—the first antipope. Thus began the great schism within the church which lasted until the early fifteenth century. Pope and antipope damned and excommunicated each other, and the church remained divided until the Council of Constance (1414-1417) restored unity to the church with one pope, in Rome.

Toward the beginning of the fifteenth century, Châteauneuf was for a time a bandits' lair. Pope Benedict XIII, in financial straits, obtained a loan from the Maréchal de Boucicaut pledging church property, including Châteauneuf, as security. Unfortunately, the marshal died and his heir, Geoffrey, an unscrupulous adventurer, inherited the mortgage. He and his band of cronies pillaged and destroyed the estates and villages throughout the region, occupying many of the châteaux, Châteauneuf among them, on the pretext of collecting what was owed him. After a long struggle the bandits were expelled by the papal troops, and the château was once again restored to the popes—or antipopes.

During the fifteenth century the castle was used from time to time as the papal residence, but gradually fell into disuse until it was more or less abandoned.

Throughout the sixteenth century religious wars raged. Châteauneuf-du-Pape joined the see of Avignon for protection, for the little good it did. In 1502 the army of the infamous Barơn des Ardets, leader of the Protestant Huguenots, burned the village of Châteauneuf. Again, in 1561, Châteauneuf was attacked, this time by the Calvinists.

The castle of Châteauneuf lay in ruins for nearly four hundred years. Only the high tower with its vaulted rooms and an expanse of wall remained standing. And so it stayed, majestically dominating the village, until 1944, when retreating Nazi troops, for no apparent reason other than to express their frustration and rage at their coming defeat, blew up the castle.

Only the façade of the castle and keep are left now of the château of the popes. Its silhouette crowns the hill, overlooking the vineyards of the southern Côtes du Rhône spread out below.

Parts of five villages are entitled to use the Châteauneuf-du-Pape appellation: Châteauneuf-du-Pape, in the southwest, with 4,992 acres (2,020 hectares) and 483 growers; Courthézon, in the east, with 1,226 acres (496 hectares), 704 growers; Orange to the north, 850 acres (344 hectares), 91 growers; Bédarrides to the southeast, 361 acres (146 hectares), 49 growers; and Sorgues to the south, with 57 acres (23 hectares) and 15 growers.

The areas covered under the AC within these villages have the same soil: a chalk and clay subsoil covered with rocks and pebbles. The vineyards on the slopes are covered with large, flat, smooth stones. These stones are less evident in the lower-lying areas. There, pebbles are more common. But what are called pebbles in Châteauneuf are called stones, small rounded stones about the size of a goose egg or a misshapen baseball over here, in the States. All the vineyards have stones of some sort.

The gentle undulating vineyards on the lower ground have red soil; beneath the surface of the hillside vineyards is blue clay. Vineyards in both areas are covered with rocks and pebbles sometimes to a depth of 5 to 6.6 feet (1.5 to 2 meters).

During the Ice Age glaciers from central Europe broke down the mountainsides carrying rocks and pebbles with them. They left the larger stones on the hills around Châteauneuf-du-Pape and smaller, more broken and worn-down rocks on the flats. Among the more impressive for the abundance of large stones are the vineyards of Domaine Mont Redon, Domaine Nalys, and Domain Vieux Télégraphe.

These stones are not just for looks; they provide good drainage for the vines and retain the heat of the day during the night. The rocks are hard on plowshares, though, which wear out frequently.

Because of the rocky soil, the vines are planted relatively wide apart. Older vines are generally spaced about 5.75 x 4.90 feet (1.75 x 1.50 meters) apart. More frequently, the spacing between vines is 5.9 x 5.9 feet (1.8 x 1.8 meters). Newer vines today are often planted 9.8 x 3.3 feet (3 x 1 meters) apart.

Over twenty-five years ago, some estates, including Château la Gardine, were granted permission to use the appellation Châteauneuf-du-Pape although they didn't have the typical Châteauneuf soil. The soil on these estates contains no clay or chalk, and there were no pebbles covering the ground. There were large rocks in the vineyards, and these were broken up into smaller stones before they could plant the vines. The soil was not totally atypical; it did contain some alluvial deposits brought down with the Alpine glaciers as in the other Châteauneuf-du-Pape vineyards.

The new plantings, granted special permission to use the Châteauneuf-du-Pape AC by the INAO, have been on land not previously planted to vines.

Part of the vineyard at Clos de l'Oratoire des Papes owned by M. Amouroux has soil similar to that of La Gardine.

In some vineyards low bushes grow among the vines. And as protection against the strong wind of the Mistral, rows of cypress trees have been planted between vineyards. In some places windbreaks made of tall reeds tied closely together shelter the vines. The Mistral, sweeping down the Rhône Valley from the north, can whip the leaves and branches of the vines about, bruising the tender fruit.

At one time olive trees were a common sight among the vines and a few of the vineyards reflect this in their names. But the devastating frost of 1956 left few remaining.

Some thirty to forty years ago Châteauneuf was known for its cherries. The village was the site of a famous cherry market. But no more—today it is the wine that brings Châteauneuf its renown.

Herbs grow wild in this area; the air is redolent with their fragrance, particularly thyme and lavender. Some people believe these herbs can be detected in the bouquet of Châteauneuf-du-Pape wine. I find the aroma of this wine quite spicy myself.

In the period after World War I viticulture in Châteauneuf was in a sad state of affairs. The wine was being bought in bulk to be used to strengthen the thinner wines of the north—notably Burgundy. (Is *that* where the Burgundies got their reputation for being big, robust wines?) Foreign grapes were being brought into Châteauneuf, and the wine sold as Châteauneuf-du-Pape. Inferior grape varieties, preferred for their greater yields, were being planted. Inevitably, the reputation of the Châteauneuf-du-Pape wine suffered.

Some of the growers approached Baron Le Roy de Boiseaumarié, who was a lawyer, to ask his help in restoring the reputation of Châteauneuf-du-Pape. Baron Le Roy had moved to Châteauneuf upon his marriage to Mlle. Bernard-Le-Saint which brought him Château Fortia, one of the most highly regarded vineyards of this region.

The Baron's plan was to protect the name of Châteauneuf-du-Pape by controlling the quality. He drew up a set of standards, rules governing the growth of the vines and the production of the wine. In 1923 he organized a group of grower-producers to put the plan into progress.

Baron Le Roy advanced the idea that the delimitation of the area should be geological rather than geographical; the nature of the soil was most important. It was felt that where the wild lavender and thyme grew together and flourished, those were the places for the vine also. Other rules limited the grape varieties and the kinds of wine (only red or white, no rosé); regulated the method of pruning and cultivation; the minimum alcoholic strength (12.5%), and rate of volatile acidity; and required the rejection of a minimum of 5% of the yield (rapé) to eliminate bad grapes. Any wine not coming up to the accepted standards would not be allowed to be named Châteauneuf-du-Pape.

It was the first time such a thing had been done, and Baron Le Roy preferred that the decision be made in the courts, rather than by the administrative authorities who would tend to be politically influenced. On June 28, 1929, the grower-producers led by Baron Le Roy won a judgment in an Orange courthouse entitling them to the protection of the law for the name Châteauneuf-du-Pape and what it stands for. Thus Châteauneuf was the first wine region in France to successfully institute strict regulations controlling the production of its wines, thanks to the efforts of Baron Le Roy.

In 1936, Senator Capus persuaded the French government to create the Comité National des Appellations d'Origine, later called the Institut National des Appellations d'Origine (INAO) to regulate the production of French wines. His plan was modeled after the standards set up by Baron Le Roy over a decade earlier.

Baron Le Roy's efforts helped to restore the prestige of Châteauneuf-du-Pape to the level it had enjoyed in the nineteenth century.

But while the Baron's work represented the first complete set of regulations on cultivation and production of Châteauneuf-du-Pape wines, they were not the first regulations on the wines of Châteauneuf-du-Pape. The first that we know of were from August 28, 1727. It was forbidden to bring in grapes from outside the wall to be used in making Châteauneuf-du-Pape wine—only grapes grown inside the walls of Châteaneuf-du-Pape could be used.

Jullien in his *Topographie de tous les vignobles* (1816), classifies Châteauneuf Calcernier (as it was then known) as first class and mentions the vineyards of De la Nerthe, La Fortia, St.-Patrice, Le Boucoup, La Jacquinotte, and Le Coteau Pierreux. In 1868 Doctor Guyot had praise for the wines of Châteauneuf, mentioning in particular De la Nerthe, Condorcet, and Vaudieu.

Just a few years later, in 1873, the plague of phylloxera destroyed the vineyards. The dead and dying vines were ripped up, and in their place wheat and fruit trees, notably almonds, apricots, and cherries, were planted.

In 1878, when the vineyards began to be replanted again, using resistant rootstock, Commandant Duclos of Château de la Nerthe set a good example with his high standards, and others followed his lead. By 1890 Châteauneuf had come a long way toward regaining its former stature once more.

The AC laws put limits on watering the vines. In dry years

the vineyards may be watered by spraying, which is uncommon, or irrigation. But the vineyard must not be submerged. The watering cannot be done more than twice, and not at all after August 15.

Rainfall in Châteauneuf-du-Pape is irregular. The land will be pummeled with heavy rains for a short period, and then receive not a drop for some time. February, July, and August are the driest months (never mind that we were drenched with rain on a day's outing during our visit in sunny July). The rainiest periods are from March to May and September to November.

One year in five the rainfall is sufficient so that the vineyards do not need to be watered. They did not in 1972, but have every year from 1973 to 1976.

More grape varieties are allowed in Châteauneuf than in any other AC above the regional ones. Perhaps Côtes du Rhône and Côtes du Rhône Villages are the only ACs in France where the vintners are allowed to use more than the thirteen varieties allowed in Châteauneuf-du-Pape.

AC law doesn't set any minimum or maximum on any of the thirteen allowable varieties, so Châteauneuf-du-Pape could be made from 100% of one grape variety or of all thirteen. In fact, few if any of the wines are made at these limits. But there is an incredible range of wine styles being produced here.

The allowable varieties: Bourboulenc—a white variety, contributing fire and brilliance, finesse and warmth; Cinsault—for bouquet, freshness, and vinosity; Clairette—a white grape, contributing characteristics similar to the Bourboulenc; Counoise—for its bouquet, freshness, suppleness, and vinosity; Grenache—for alcohol, smoothness, softness, sweetness, and warmth, and for making a quicker-maturing wine; Mourvèdre—for body, color, and firmness; Muscardin—

for characteristics similar to the Mourvèdre; Picardan; Pic-poul—for characteristics similar to the Counoise; Roussanne—a white variety; Syrah—for body, deep color, and staying power; Terret noir—for increasing the quantity (this plant is a prolific producer); and Vaccarèse—like Syrah, for body, deep color, and staying power.

At the end of the nineteenth century the classic blend of grape varieties was, according to information compiled by Commandant Duclos: 20% Grenache, Cinsault (alcohol, smoothness, and warmth); 30% Mourvèdre, Syrah, Muscardin, Vaccarèse (color, flavor, longevity, and sturdiness); 40% Counoise, Picpoul (charm, freshness, bouquet, and suppleness); 10% Clairette, Bourboulenc (white varieties—fire, brilliance, and elegance).

It is claimed that the best wines are those which combine all thirteen varieties. But very few producers now use all thirteen in their wines.

Today the most common variety is the Grenache, but contrary to most reports, its use is on the decline not the increase. At one time, because of the high sugar levels in this grape variety, and the consequently high alcohol in its wine, Grenache was more widely planted.

It's no secret that Châteauneuf-du-Pape used to be added to the wines of Burgundy to strengthen them, just as Hermitage was used in Bordeaux for the same reason. The higher alcohol that the Grenache gave the wine was a desirable feature. Fifty years ago approximately 90% of the plantings in Châteauneuf were Grenache. Today this has shrunk to 60-65%. Consequently, today's Châteauneuf-du-Pape, although high in alcohol for a table wine by any standards, is somewhat lower than it used to be.

Minimum for the appellation is 12.5%, the highest in

France, and shared with very few other wines (Gigondas and Côtes du Rhône Villages have the same minimum). More commonly, though, Châteauneuf-du-Pape achieves 13.6 to 13.8%, and over 14% is not unusual. Even the white wine must be 12.5%, although this wine generally comes closer to 13%.

Because the vintners are aiming at fruitier wines today, plantings of Cinsault, Mourvèdre, Muscardin, and Syrah are increasing; Picardin and Terret noir are being planted less and less, and possibly within a few years will all but disappear.

The INAO has promoted Cinsault because it is a low-alcohol grape, and it felt that Châteauneuf-du-Pape was too high in alcohol. But INAO has set the 12.5% alcoholic minimum. The Châteauneuf producers tend not to favor Cinsault, as they need higher-alcohol grapes to meet the minimum. And some growers feel that the Cinsault is an inferior variety because of its thin skin, which makes it susceptible to disease.

All varieties except the Syrah are head pruned, giving the vines the appearance of little bushes. Syrah, because of its long bunches and its need for more sunlight, is trained on wires. This makes it easy to pick out in the Châteauneuf-du-Pape vineyards.

White Châteauneuf-du-Pape wine can be made from Grenache blanc, Clairette blanc, Picpoul, Bourboulenc, Roussanne, Terret blanc. Many producers use only two or three varieties. Clairette blanc produces a sturdy wine; Grenache blanc adds bouquet.

White Châteauneuf-du-Pape was first made at the request of the popes. They found the red wine, often approaching 15% alcohol, too heavy at the first mass in the morning. So they requested a lighter, white wine for the service. White Châteauneuf is still sometimes referred to as *vin de messe* ("wine of the mass").

The makeup of some leading Châteauneuf-du-Pape estates:

Domaine Mont Redon—Grenache 60-70%, Syrah 10-15%, Cinsault 10-15%, Mourvèdre 5%, others (nine remaining allowable varieties) 5%.

Château Fortia (red)—Grenache 70%, Syrah 15-18%, Mourvèdre 5%, the remainder is comprised of the other ten varieties.

Château Fortia (white)—Clairette blanc 70-75%, Roussanne 20-25%, Grenache blanc 5%.

Château de la Gardine—Grenache 66%, Syrah 23%, Mourvèdre 8%, Clairette 3%.

Les Cailloux (white)—Clairette blanc 95%, Bourboulenc 5%.

Chante Perdrix—Grenache 86%, Cinsault 5-6%, Syrah 5-6%, Muscardin 3%.

Chante Cigale—Grenache 80%, Syrah 12%, Cinsault 5%, Mourvèdre 3%.

Normally the harvest in Châteauneuf begins about the middle of September and goes on until the middle of October.

Appellation sets a maximum of 375 gallons/acre (35 hectoliters/hectare). Total yield, though, may exceed this by 20%, or 450 gallons/acre (42 hectoliters/hectare), but the excess is declassified to *vin ordinaire*. If the maximum plus 20% is exceeded, the entire crop will be denied the Châteauneuf-du-Pape AC. In the case of a yield such as this, the grower most likely won't pick the excess, leaving it on the vines for the birds.

Additionally, at least 5% of the 375 gallons/acre must be rejected—the *rapé*—and 10% isn't uncommon. The idea behind the *rapé*, and the way it works in practice, is that the growers will reject the bad grapes and use only good-quality fruit for their Châteauneuf-du-Pape wine.

The *rapé* may be used for *vin ordinaire*. The workers often receive a provision of this ordinary wine as part of their contract. Some drink it as their daily wine; others sell it. This wine is frequently kept in a fiberglass tank fitted with a floating cap. As the wine is drawn out, the cap sinks, thereby preventing air from coming in contact with, and hurting, the wine.

The Fédération des Syndicats des Producteurs de Châteauneuf-du-Pape meets each year to decide upon the maximum yield for that vintage. AC laws allow the maximum to be adjusted according to conditions. The Syndicat can only lower the 375 gallon/acre (35 hectoliters/hectare) maximum, though; it can never increase it. The 20% over maximum allowance applies only to the years' maximum yield, not to the 375 gallon/acre maximum. In 1968, for example, the Syndicat set a 278 gallon/acre (26 hectoliters/hectare) maximum.

If a grower picked over 332 gallons/acre (31 hectoliters/hectare), the entire vineyard was declassified. In 1968, which was plagued by poor weather, there was a problem of rot in the vineyards, and many growers rejected more than the normal 5 to 10% *rapé*.

The current Syndicat of growers was formed in 1963. The first Syndicat had been founded thirty years earlier. Its aim is to defend the reputation of Châteauneuf-du-Pape and help the growers improve their quality. It has a modern laboratory. By far the great majority of the growers belong to the Syndicat. Qualified members are granted permission to use the bottle with the papal coat of arms which is embossed on the glass. This symbol with its crossed keys and papal miter has been the property of the Syndicat since 1939. Fifths and magnums, but not tenths, bear the coat of arms—the tenth size being too small, according to the bottle company. The official Châteauneuf-du-Pape bottle bearing this seal was defined by a decree of November 2, 1966.

Besides the Syndicat, there is a union of growers who have joined together to improve the quality of their wine. The Reflets de Châteauneuf-du-Pape, founded in 1954, is not a cooperative. Each member makes his own wine, but bottles and stores it in the cellar of the Reflets, which has enough room for 100,000 bottles. In this way the members have access to better equipment and perhaps better storage conditions than each individual would have on his own.

Each member is assessed according to his production, since the larger his production, the more he makes use of the facilities. Presently this assessment is just under one franc per bottle (about 15 cents).

Wines bottled at the Reflets bear the words *mise en bouteille aux Reflets* ("bottled at the Reflets") and each bottle is numbered.

The current members, all highly respected producers, of the Caves Reflets de Châteauneuf-du-Pape: Lucien Brunel (Les Cailloux), Charles Descarrega (Les Cabanes), Pierre Lancon (La Solitude), Nicolet Frères (Chante Perdrix), Joseph Sabon (Clos du Mont Olivet), and Roger Sabon (Les Olivets). Some of the best as well as some of my favorite Châteauneuf-du-Pape wines are produced by these estates.

Some seven or eight years ago, another group similar to the Reflets was formed. This cooperative bottling and storage cellar has ten or eleven members.

Other than these two cooperative cellars and the

Coopérative des Producteurs de Châteauneuf-du-Pape (Chapter 3), there are no other cooperative cellars in Châteauneuf. In fact, there is no true co-op, which makes the wine, bottles it, and sells it under the name of the co-op. This is quite unusual in the southern Côtes du Rhône, where growers' cooperatives are commonplace.

Other highly regarded producers: Baron Le Roy (Château Fortia); Jacques Mousset (Domaine des Fines Roches); Remy Diffonty (Cuvée du Vatican); Paul Jean (Réserve du Capitole); Philippe Dufays (Domaine de Nalys); SCI Les 3 Domaines; Berard Père et Fils (La Terre Ferme); Henri Brunier (Domaine du Vieux Télégraphe); Paul Coulon (Domaine de Beaurenard); Jean Claude Sabon; Jean Versino; Jean Trintignant (Domaine Trintignant); Joseph Marchand (Domaine de Boisdauphin); Pierre Usseglio (Route de Courthézon); Etienne Grangeon (Domaine du Christia); Jean Deydier (Les Clefs d'Or); Jean Pierre Boisson; Elie Armenier; Paul Avril (Clos des Papes); Pierre Barrot; Jacques Mestre; Jean Abeille (Domaine de Mont Redon); Jacques Perrin (Domaine de Beaucastel); André Berard; Joseph Boiron; Maurice Mayard; Paul Royer; Pierre Sabon; Pierre Raynaud (Domaine des Sénéchaux); Régis Chaston (Rue des Mimosas); Henri Jourdan (Le Vieux Moulin); Domaine de la Nerthe; Gaston Brunel (Domaine de la Gardine); André Drapery (Domaine du Grand Goulet); Pierre Quiot (Château Maucoil); René Laugier (Domaine de la Roquette); Louis Arnaud (Domaine Cabrières-les-Silex); M. Serre (Domaine de St.-Préfert); Gabriel Meffre (Château de Vadieu).

Some notable estates not already listed: Domaine de Cabrières; Château de la Fond du Pape; Mas St.-Louis; Domaine Condorcet; Château Rayas; Château St.-Patrice; Côte Brulée; Domaine du Télégraphe; Clos St.-Pierre; Clos des Patriciens; Domaine de la Font du Loup; Clos de l'Oratoire des Papes; Domaine le Clos; Domaine de Boucou; Domaine le Grand Gardiole.

Some important estates with respect to size: Domaine Mont Redon—222.4 acres (90 hectares); Domaine de la Nerthe—134.5 acres (54.42 hectares); Château de la Gardine—133.4 acres (54 hectares); Domaine de Nalys—115 acres (46.54 hectares); Clos Saint Jean—93.9 acres (38 hectares); Domaine des Fines Roches—84.8 acres (34.33 hectares); Clos des Papes—76.6 acres (31 hectares); Château de Vaudieu—73.4 acres (29.70 hectares); Domaine des Sénéchaux—72.4 acres (29.3 hectares); Château Fortia—67.7 acres (27.4 hectares); Chapoutier, La Bernadine—66.7 acres (27 hectares); Chante Perdrix—44.5 acres (18 hectares); Domaine de Saint Préfert—39.5 acres (16 hectares).

The local wine fraternity of Châteauneuf-du-Pape, the Echansonnerie des Papes (Cupbearers of the Popes), holds its ceremonies in the former pontifical cellar. The château tower used to be the scene of the festivities, but since the bombing, the cellar has been restored to the way it was in the fourteenth century so that the ceremonies can be held there.

The castle cellar is also where the yearly festival of Saint Marc, the patron saint of Châteauneuf-du-Pape, is celebrated. About one-third of the grower-producers (making about 150) gather on April 25 to taste the year-old wines and also three-year-old reds. This festival has been held every year since 1966. Originally a one-year-old red, a one-year-old white, and any older wine of the producer's choice were evaluated. But because of the diversity of vintages, this last category was changed a few years ago to a three-year-old red, which makes comparison more meaningful.

The following list names the winners of this blind tasting. Since only about 150 grower-producers submit their wines, no real conclusion about Châteauneuf-du-Pape as a whole can be drawn. Some really fine producers don't enter. But it is interesting to learn the wines that have done well.

SAINT MARC's, 1976

New Wine (1975): First Prize—Remy Diffonty; Second Prize—Paul Jean; Third Prize—Philippe Dufays.

White Wine (1975): First Prize—Paul Jean; Second Prize—SCI Les 3 Domaines; Third Prize—Berard Père et Fils.

Old Wine (1972): First Prize—Henri Brunier; Second Prize—Paul Coulon; Third Prize—Jean Claude Sabon.

SAINT MARC's, 1975

New Wine (1974): First Prize—Jean Claude Sabon; Second Prize—Paul Coulon; Third Prize—Jean Versino.

White Wine (1974): First Prize—Philippe Dufays; Second Prize—Jean Trintignant.

Old Wine (1971): First Prize—Jean Claude Sabon; Second Prize—Joseph Sabon; Third Prize—Joseph Marchand.

SAINT MARC's, 1974

New Wine (1973): First Prize—Jacques Perrin; Second Prize—Berard Père et Fils; Third Prize—Paul Jean.

White Wine (1973): First Prize—Philippe Dufays; Second Prize—André Berard.

Old Wine: First Prize—Jean Claude Sabon (vintage 1971); Second Prize—Philippe Dufays (vintage 1969); Third Prize—Henri Brunier (vintage 1970).

SAINT MARC's, 1973

New Wine (1972): First Prize—Jean Versino; Second Prize—Pierre Barrot; Third Prize—Paul Coulon.

White Wine (1972): First Prize—Jacques Mestre; Second Prize—Etienne Grangeon; Third Prize—Philippe Dufays.

Old Wine: First Prize—Jean Claude Sabon (vintage 1970);

Second Prize—Domaine de Mont Redon (vintage 1962);
Third Prize—Nicolet Frères (vintage 1970).

SAINT MARC'S, 1972

New Wine (1971): First Prize—Pierre Usseglio; Second Prize—Paul Coulon; Third Prize—Philippe Dufays.

White Wine (1971): First Prize—Etienne Grangeon; Second Prize—Jean Deydier; Third Prize—Paul Coulon.

Old Wine (1970): First Prize—Jean Pierre Boisson; Second Prize—Elie Armenier; Third Prize—Jean Avril.

SAINT MARC'S, 1971

New Wine (1970): First Prize—Paul Coulon; Second Prize—Pierre Sabon; Third Prize—Pierre Raynaud.

White Wine (1970): First Prize—Etienne Grangeon.

Old Wine (1967): First Prize— Régis Chaston; Second Prize—Barrot Frères; Third Prize—Henri Jourdan.

SAINT MARC'S, 1970

New Wine (1969): First Prize—Paul Coulon; Second Prize—Pierre Sabon; Third Prize—Joseph Sabon.

White Wine (1969): First Prize—Berard Père et Fils.

SAINT MARC'S, 1969

New Wine (1968): First Prize—Paul Coulon; Second Prize—Paul Royer; Third Prize—Barrot Frères.

White Wine (1968): First Prize—Berard Père et Fils.

SAINT MARC'S, 1967

New Wine (1966): First Prize—Joseph Sabon; Second Prize—Maurice Mayard; Third Prize—Jean Claude Sabon.

SAINT MARC'S, 1966

New Wine (1965): First Prize—Paul Avril; Second Prize—Barrot Frères; Third Prize—Joseph Boiron.

Châteauneuf-du-Pape is about 98% red wine and 2% white wine—it can never be rosé. The red Châteauneuf is made in two basic styles: the traditional style, which produces a big, deep-colored, robust, and tannic wine requiring perhaps seven to eight years to achieve full maturity, and capable of living for a decade or two afterward; and a newer style, which is less alcoholic, fresher, and when young, fruitier and softer. This wine matures quickly and then passes into old age and feebleness quite quickly. It is at its best from one to three years after the vintage and won't live much beyond.

This newer style is made, according to the argument advanced, in response to consumer demand for faster-maturing wines, which don't require cellar space or time to become ready.

But for those consumers who want that kind of wine, there is Beaujolais. This newer style of Châteauneuf lacks the charm and grace of Beaujolais. It is awkward because of its softness and high alcohol, which don't complement each other.

There are enough lovers of the traditional Châteauneuf-du-Pape, I think, who are not in a hurry and are willing to find room in their never-big-enough wine cellars or wine closets for a traditional Châteauneuf worth waiting for. Perhaps the real reason for the change of style has more to do with the fact that the newer style can be produced more cheaply and sold more quickly (as it requires little or no barrel aging).

But for those who like it (*chacun à son goût*), look to Domaine Nalys, which perhaps best typifies this fresh, fruity style.

The traditional Châteauneuf-du-Pape is fermented in contact with the skins and some of the stems for three to four weeks. This, of course, imparts more tannin and more of everything else to the wine. The wine is then left to rest in wooden casks for two to five years. Some producers have been known to leave the wine in barrel until it is sold, at which time it is bottled. Noël Sabon of Chante Cigale is reputed to have bottled some of his 1964 after it had been in wood for a decade.

The newer style of Châteaneuf-du-Pape is fermented by a semi-carbonic maceration method. The whole grape bunches, unbroken, are put for about eight days in closed cement vats, perhaps as large as 700 gallons. The weight of the bunches at the top presses some of the juice out of the grapes below, which begins to ferment. Fermentation releases carbon dioxide, which builds up pressure in the closed vat until it causes the fermentation to stop. The partially fermented must macerates the grapes.

After this initial step, the bunches are removed, pressed, and fermented.

These wines are matured for as little as three to four months on up to a year in stainless steel, glass, or cement. They will not see wood.

When they are bottled, they are quite fresh and fruity. In another year or two they will lose their freshness and their fruitiness.

This new method of fermentation was introduced into Châteauneuf-du-Pape over twenty years ago, and the number of producers using it is unfortunately increasing.

A number of producers, like Château Fines Roches, make part of their wine by carbonic maceration and part in the traditional style. They blend the two wines together to produce a fuller, but faster-maturing and fruitier wine. I still prefer the good old fashioned traditional style, but have tasted some fine Châteauneuf-du-Papes made in this manner.

Some producers in Châteauneuf-du-Pape who use carbonic maceration ferment their wine for longer than the usual length of time. These wines, surprisingly, can be quite long-lived.

Some of the producers who use the longer fermentation, such as M. Lucien Brunel and his son André, contend that there are not two methods of fermentation in Châteauneuf, but three: traditional, standard carbonic maceration, and the longer carbonic maceration. Their viewpoint is that the longer-lived wine produced by the twenty-one-day fermentation by carbonic maceration is a different type of wine from the regular carbonic maceration and should be considered as a separate type.

In the early 1950s M. Charnay from the INAO encouraged the first experiments with carbonic maceration in Châteauneuf. In 1952 a few producers, including Lucien Brunel (Les Cailloux) and Joseph Sabon (Mont Olivet), made some wine using the carbonic maceration method. The Les Cailloux Cuvée Paule was fermented for twenty-one days with carbonic maceration. This cuvée was kept separate, and according to André Brunel the wine is still good.

M. Dufays (Domaine Nalys), on the other hand, using the regular carbonic maceration method, ferments his wine for ten days. His wines are best from their first to their third year.

Lucien Brunel believes that some vineyards yield grapes that can produce good wines with the carbonic maceration method, while other vineyards cannot. Soil, Brunel points out, is the determining factor. The soil should be less rocky and have a higher proportion of clay, with some chalk beneath. The vineyard should have pebbles but not a lot.

Joseph Sabon, whose wines often win at the Saint Marc festival, is reputedly an expert on matching the grapes and the soil to the method of fermentation—traditional or carbonic maceration. Sabon's sons, Jean Claude, Pierre, and Roger, use the same method as their father. The Sabon family is among the most highly regarded producers in Châteauneuf, proving, I guess, that if handled right carbonic maceration can result in a good Châteauneuf wine.

A number of growers, the smaller ones in particular, have scattered holdings throughout Châteauneuf-du-Pape. As it is naturally more work to maintain separated vineyards, it's not uncommon for growers to trade parcels to consolidate their holdings.

Alphonse Daudet, the noted French novelist, described Châteauneuf-du-Pape as the wine of kings. Others have called this robust red the king of wines.

One thing for sure, Châteauneuf-du-Pape—the traditional type, now—is robust in body and full in flavor. The strength of this wine has been attributed to the soil (sturdy as a rock?). When mature these wines will be soft and flavorful, with good fruit. The bouquet of Châteauneuf-du-Pape evokes the aroma of herbs and spices. Some imaginative writers have described it as a bouquet of oriental spices! Others say the bouquet brings up truffles.

Châteauneuf-du-Pape requires a full-flavored meat such as game or pot-roasted beef to do justice to the wine, which in turn complements this food. Wild boar, for those who can find it, comes highly recommended. And I wouldn't dispute it, never having had the chance myself to dine on that rather exotic beast.

The white Châteauneuf-du-Pape is a full-bodied, manly wine, which although strong is not coarse. (No offense to the women's libbers, who may think of it as amazonlike, rather than manly, if they wish.) It has a distinctive, dry flavor which some find reminiscent of gunflint (those must be the hunters of wild boar). Its bouquet, like the red, brings up herbs and spices. This wine improves in the bottle for a few years. Its only defect, perhaps, is low acidity, making the wine somewhat awkward, or heavy. It goes well with pork, veal, or turkey.

Vintage Evaluation:

1975 Below-average quality, although some good wines were made. Production was much below average.

1974 Similar to 1973; not a vintage to keep.

1973 A light, uneven, fast-maturing vintage of poor to average quality; fruity and agreeable, but not to keep.

1972 A vintage to age. Very small yield. This underrated vintage produced some excellent wines that will improve for some time.

1971 A very good to excellent vintage; very well-balanced wines. The traditional wines are continuing to improve.

1970 A prolific vintage, which produced good wines that were elegant but not as long-lived as the 1972s, although the better ones are by no means ready yet.

1969 An uneven year which saw some very good and some rather poor wines; those from the better estates can be excellent.

1968 A failure.

1967 An excellent year. The traditional wines are long-lived. There is some disagreement over which was better, 1966 or 1967; generally, I prefer the '67s.

1966 Very good. Not so good as '67 according to some growers, but better according to others. These wines—the better ones—are at their peak now; the lesser ones are gone.

1965 Fair.

1964 An excellent vintage for some, average for others—
uneven. Those '64s remaining should be drunk up
now as they won't last.

1963 Mediocre.

1962 A very good vintage; some estates produced better
wine than in 1961. These wines are at their best
now.

1961 Less good than suggested at the time, but outstanding
nevertheless. Some excellent bottles can still be
found. They are holding well; no need to drink
them up right away, they will last.

Older vintages that were outstanding: 1947, 1952, 1955,
1957. The best of these can still be quite good, but it's
chancy.

Excellent white wines were produced in 1970 and 1971,
with the '70s more elegant and faster-maturing. While the
red wines in 1973 were uneven, the whites were excellent.
Some producers rate the 1973 whites as the best of the past
decade.

Three years ago, Gaston Brunel of Château de la Gardine
and Jean Abeille of Domaine Mont Redon got together with
about one hundred other growers to form the Hospice de
Châteauneuf-du-Pape. The brainchild of M. Brunel, the
hospice is based on the idea of the Hospice de Beaune. The
Hospice de Châteauneuf-du-Pape, though, is not a hospital,
but a home for the aged.

Every grower in Châteauneuf was asked to contribute a
portion of his crop to the Hospice; about one hundred did.
Each grower who belongs to the federation contributes a part
of his harvested grapes. The wine is then made, under the
control of the federation of growers.

In 1973, their first year, the wine was made at Domaine Mont Redon. Félicien Diffonty, mayor of Châteauneuf and a highly respected producer, of Cuvée du Vatican, made the 1974 wine. In 1975, Henri Jourdan made the special cuvée. M. Jourdan now will continue making and aging the wine.

The wine is made in the traditional style, and is to be a typical example of red Châteauneuf-du-Pape; no white will be made. Each year, 25,000 to 30,000 numbered bottles of this special wine will be made to support the Hospice de Châteauneuf-du-Pape. The 1973 production was 28,000 bottles. The 1974 has been bottled. The 1975 was not bottled, but sold to shippers.

Châteauneuf-du-Pape has two restaurants listed in the Michelin Guide Rouge, one worth a visit, the other not. Château Fines Roches, a restaurant with its own vineyard, is in a picturesque medieval-style castle surrounded with vines. Fines Roches offers fine food, including some local specialties. It also has an excellent selection of local wines, some dating back to 1952, which are reasonably priced. The decor is elegant; the service, friendly and efficient.

One cannot say the same for La Mule du Pape. There, the food is of mediocre to average quality, and the service slow and inattentive. The prices seem outrageously high for the quality and quantity, and you may find hidden charges when the check comes. One wonders how long it has been since the Michelin rater ate here. Best avoided.

La Mère Germaine, the town's only hotel with a grand total of three rooms, has a good restaurant. Although not as good as Fines Roches, it is in a more moderate price category. Portions are large. The service, though unprofessional, is willing.

Le Pistou is another restaurant in Châteauneuf worth a visit. As the name implies, it specializes in pistou, the vegetable soup of Provence flavored with garlic and the marvelously aromatic fresh basil grown in pots on the terrace.

In nearby Avignon, La Fourchette is a good place to dine. This small restaurant is a bit crowded, but for good reason. The cuisine is very good to excellent, as is the service. And the prices are very reasonable. Reservations are recommended.

At the restaurant in the Hôtel de l'Europe, also in Avignon, the food and the service are spotty; the prices, high. Best avoided.

The Père Anselme Museum in Châteauneuf displays an interesting collection of old bottles, a sixteenth-century wine press, old crushers and plows, and other winemaking curiosities.

The view from the ruins of the pope's new castle offers a panorama to warm the cockles of a wine lover's heart. There beyond the pink tiled roofs of the village are the vineyards, a deep green sea of vines rippling out in all directions.

18. COTES DU RHONE VILLAGES

In recognition of the superior quality and reputation of certain wine villages in the Côtes du Rhône, a ministerial decree was issued allowing them to append their village names to AC Côtes du Rhône. The four villages recognized in 1953 under this special decree were Gigondas and Cairanne in the department of Vaucluse, and Chusclan and Laudun in the department of Gard. In 1955, Vacqueyras and in 1957, Vinsobres were added.

In August 1967, AC Côtes du Rhône Villages was created. This new AC allowed additional villages to append their names to Côtes du Rhône, as had been done before, and also defined significantly more stringent standards under the Villages AC than are required under AC Côtes du Rhône.

While AC Côtes du Rhône allows 535 gallons/acre (50 hectoliters/hectare) maximum yield, the Côtes du Rhône Villages allows only 375 gallons/acre (35 hectoliters/hectare). Under special circumstances this maximum can be increased to 450 gallons/acre (42 hectoliters/hectare) but INAO must grant special authorization for this, after checking the wines and verifying the quality. As in Châteauneuf-du-Pape and Gigondas, a portion of the grapes harvested must be rejected (the *rapé*). This encourages the selection of the best grapes, thereby improving the quality of the wine.

If the yield exceeds 535 gallons/acre (50 hectoliters/hectare), the entire harvest from that vineyard is declassified,

171

with 535 gallons/acre being allowed the simple Côtes du Rhône AC and the rest sold as *vin ordinaire.*

If the yield is 535 gallons/acre or less, up to 375 gallons/ acre (35 hectoliters/hectare) will be allowed the Côtes du Rhône Villages name, assuming that all other requirements for Côtes du Rhône Villages are met, and the remainder allowed to be labeled simply Côtes du Rhône.

Côtes du Rhône Villages red can be made from up to 65% Grenache noir, and must contain at least 10% Syrah and no less than 15% Mourvèdre and Cinsault, singularly or together. All other varieties allowed under AC Côtes du Rhône may be used up to a maximum of 10%: Clairette, Terret noir, Picardan, Roussette or Roussanne, Marsanne, Bourboulenc, Viognier, Carignan, Counoise, Muscardin, Vaccarèse, Pinot fin de Bourgogne, Mauzac, Pascal blanc, Ugni blanc, Calitor, Gamay noir á jus blanc, and Camarèse.

Since the introduction of the Syrah grape, the quality of these wines has improved. Plantings of Syrah are now increasing at the expense of Grenache and some of the lesser-known, and lesser, varieties.

The Villages rosé must use at least 15% Camarèse and/or Cinsault, and no more than 60% Grenache. The other Côtes du Rhône varieties, any or all, are allowed up to 10%.

Côtes du Rhône Villages white must contain no less than 80% of one or more of the following three varieties: Clairette, Bourboulenc, Roussanne. Grenache blanc may not exceed 10% nor may any of the other allowable Côtes du Rhône varieties.

French-American hybrid grape varieties are not allowed. If hybrids are found in any vineyard, the entire output of that vineyard is declassified to *vin ordinaire.* (Interestingly enough, some American wine growers have been touting hybrid varieties over the European vinifera varieties, especially on the East Coast. Perhaps the wise old French know something we don't.)

As with Châteauneuf-du-Pape, Gigondas, and a few other local appellations, irrigation is permitted for Côtes du Rhône Villages wines twice, but only in very dry years.

Vinification must follow local customs. And under no circumstances is chaptalization permitted. Red wines must achieve at least 12.5% alcohol, the same high level as Châteauneuf-du-Pape and Gigondas. Rosé and white wines must not be less than 12%.

Actually, lowering this minimum might provide for more enjoyable wines in my opinion. Some of them are really just a bit *too* high in alcohol. This high alcohol adds to the robustness of these wines, but for those that are most enjoyable when young the high alcohol detracts.

All wines, to be awarded the Côtes du Rhône Villages AC, must be tasted for quality and approved by a committee of the INAO.

AC Côtes du Rhône Villages on a label without the village name is an indication that the wine is a blend of two or more villages.

Village names you might see appended to Côtes du Rhône: Cairanne, Gigondas, Rasteau, Roaix, Séguret, Vacqueyras, Valréas, and Visan in the Vaucluse; Chusclan and Laudun in the Gard; Rochegude, Rousset-les-Vignes, St.-Maurice-sur-Eygues, St.-Pantaléon-les-Vignes, and Vinsobres in the Drôme.

The region of the Côtes du Rhône Villages is dotted with reminders of bygone days—Roman ruins and hillside villages of ancient houses encircled by medieval ramparts and crowded for protection at the foot of a centuries-old church or the ruins of a once-proud château.

Vineyards and orchards, and sometimes both—trees growing in among the vines—cornfields, woodlands, and scraggly hills make up the pleasant, pastoral countryside.

COTES DU RHONE VILLAGES (DROME)

The Drôme villages entitled to use the Côtes du Rhône Villages AC stretch from the boundaries of the Dauphiné and the Comtat de Venaissin almost to Vaison-la-Romaine.

The soil here is poor and dry, but the wines are fruity and forthright. The highly regarded rosé and the somewhat more popular red are enjoyable when young, and generally at their best within a few years of the vintage.

The five villages, from north to south, authorized to use this AC are Rousset-les-Vignes, St.-Pantaléon-les-Vignes (a village with an eleventh-century Romanesque church), Vinsobres, St.-Maurice-sur-Eygues, and Rochegude.

Vinsobres is the most highly regarded of the Côtes du Rhône villages of Drôme. Vines here are planted on terraced slopes. The climate is not so hot as in the other villages, especially those in Vaucluse and Gard to the south.

These red wines are less alcoholic than those from the southern villages. They are relatively long-lasting but already quite enjoyable in their third year.

Some noteworthy growers: Cave du Prieuré, Fernand Durma, Jaume Père et Fils, Jean Vinson.

COTES DU RHONE VILLAGES (VAUCLUSE)

Also on the east bank of the Rhône are the wine villages of the Vaucluse department. Most of these villages are between Bollene (to the northwest), Vaison-la-Romaine (northeast), Carpentras (southeast), and Orange (southwest). Valréas, the northernmost village, and Visan, just to the south, are north of the general boundaries. The other villages are Roaix, Rasteau, Cairanne, Séguret, Sablet, Gigondas, Vacqueyras, and Sarrians.

In the Vaucluse villages vines are planted on slopes in chalky, clay soil. The vineyards as they have been extended have edged the wild herbs, thyme and lavender, to the hilltops. The vines stretch across the Vaucluse right to the foot of Mt. Ventoux, the region's highest mountain.

The wines of these villages are strong, robust, and fruity, high in alcohol and sometimes low in acidity. With few exceptions these wines are best before their fifth year and can be enjoyed in their second or third.

Valréas is a picturesque walled village with eleventh-century houses perched on the side of the hill. Valréas is in a rather unusual situation being in the department of Vaucluse but entirely surrounded by the department of Drôme. This was papal territory at one time, as reflected in the co-op name, Union des Vignerons de l'Enclave des Papes à Valréas, but reunited with France since the revolution.

Besides the growers cooperative other notable producers include Romain Bouchard (Domaine du Val des Rois), Henri Davin (Domaine de la Prevosse), André Gras (Domaine St.-Chetin), Leo Roussin (Domaine de la Fuzière), André Sayn, and René Sinard (Domaine des Grands Devers).

The vast majority of the approximately 370 growers of *Visan* belong to the local cooperative, founded in 1925. Domaine de Coste-Chaude is a highly respected independent grower-producer of Visan red and rosé.

Sablet, a village of about 1,000 inhabitants still surrounded by its medieval ramparts, boasts a Romanesque church from the twelfth and fourteenth centuries.

This village is entitled to label its wines Côtes du Rhône Visan, if they meet the AC standards.

Louis Chamfort and Luc Arene (Domaine de la Marsanne) are respected producers.

Roaix was founded in the twelfth century by the Knights Templar. Most of the growers here own small parcels of land and belong to the local cooperative, Les Vignerons de Roaix-Séguret. The co-op is shared with Séguret, Roaix's neighbor to the south. These two villages lie between Rasteau, Vaison-la-Romaine, and Gigondas.

Most of the fruity, robust wine here is red, although some rosé is produced.

Lambert Florimond is a highly regarded independent producer.

Séguret is a picturesque little village (population 800) with medieval houses, a twelfth-century church, and the ruins of a feudal castle from the same century.

The hillside restaurant, La Table du Comtat, is a good place to enjoy the local wines accompanied by good regional cuisine. It also offers a panorama of the plains of the Comtat Venaissin stretching for miles below, out to the Dentelles de Montmirail, part of the Massif Central, and the Alps beyond.

Like Roaix, most of the local wine in Séguret is red, stong, and fruity.

Rasteau has a local AC for its *vin doux naturel* and *vin de liqueur,* and a Village AC for its other wine. (See Chapter 12.)

Cairanne, a small hillside village surrounded by a sea of vines, offers much of interest to the traveler. The Knights Templar built the fortress here with its ramparts, tower, and dungeon, the scene of much bloodshed during the many religious wars of the Middle Ages. A magnificent panorama of the surrounding countryside can be enjoyed from its high tower. Cairanne has a museum of wine with artifacts and relics. Documents show that wine has been made here since at least the Middle Ages. A neolithic cemetery has also been discovered here.

Hannibal is believed to have passed close by Cairanne on his route south over the Alps.

Vines are planted on the slopes facing due south. There is some terracing in the steeper vineyards.

Generally the grapes are harvested in Cairanne about September 20 to 30.

Cairanne also produces a *vin doux naturel,* not covered under AC regulations. The grapes for this wine are normally harvested about a month later. The grapes used for the VDN are planted on the upper slopes, where they receive maximum sunshine.

In 1938 Cairanne was granted permission to produce a *vin doux naturel.* Besides the cooperative, only Mme. Lebre and Alary et Fils (L'Oratoire St.-Martin) are allowed to make a VDN in Cairanne.

The Cave Coopérative des Coteaux de Cairanne was founded in 1929. M. Lacrotte, the president, is also president of the GIE Présence des Côtes du Rhône (Rhônecote), discussed in Chapter 3.

The grapes for the *vin doux*—100% Grenache—are harvested when they have attained sufficient sugar to achieve 14.5% alcohol. But the fermentation is not allowed to finish; to produce a wine that will be sweet, brandy is added to the fermenting must to arrest fermentation and retain some of the sugar. The alcoholic content is increased to 16-16.5%. The wine is then aged in small brandy casks.

This VDN is made every year by the co-op. It is never vintage-dated, but is frequently the product of a single year. Sometimes vintages are blended, but not often. Cairanne *vin doux naturel* is red in color. It is sweeter than the VDN of Rasteau. This sweetness, though, is balanced quite well by its acidity. It is more "madeirized" (*rancio*) both in aroma and flavor than the regular *vin doux* of Rasteau. This is a good wine, well chilled, with fruit or nuts, after dinner, or before, as an aperitif.

Of the 1,320,000 to 1,508,220 gallons (50,000-57,000 hectoliters) of wine annually produced by the co-op, 10,584 to 26,460 gallons (400 to 1,000 hectoliters) are VDN, about 26,460 gallons (1,000 hectoliters) are white, and from 79,380 to 132,300 gallons (3,000 to 5,000 hectoliters) are rosé. The remainder is red.

The co-op uses basket presses and ferments its wines in cement tanks. The wines are aged in Russian oak casks. The co-op is very modern looking except for those presses.

Customers bring in their jugs to the co-op to be filled from the tanks by hoses. You almost expect to hear someone say, "Fill 'er up."

Besides the cooperative, Alary, and Lebre, Cairanne wines are also produced by Bardelli (Clos Bellevue), Beaumet (Domaine St.-Andéol), Brusset (Domaine des Travers), De-lubac Père et Fils (Domaine de la Fauconnière), Grignan (Domaine du Grand Jas), Pierrefeu (Domaine Le Plaisir), Rabasse-Charavin (Les Coteaux St. Martin), and Zanti-Cumino (Domaine de Banvin).

Gigondas was awarded its own local AC in 1971 (see Chapter 16, Gigondas).

Vacqueyras, to the south of Gigondas, is surrounded by the ruins of its medieval ramparts. Its church goes back to the eleventh century. Many Roman relics and artifacts—urns, medallions, and coins—have been unearthed in the neighborhood.

Wine has been made here since at least the twelfth century, when troubadour Raimbaut sang its praises. Pope Clement VI sent his monks to Vacqueyras to help with the harvest.

Documents show that this small village of only about 800 inhabitants was the site of an eighteenth-century wine fair. Since 1973 Vacqueyras has had a modern wine fair, first held in the spring, but now every summer.

The local cooperative, founded in 1957, has over 100 members. Its brand name is Le Vin du Troubadour. This co-op produces one-third to one-half of the wines of Vacqueyras.

Some fifty independent producers make wine here. Among the better known are Archimbaud (Clos des Cazaux), Bernard (Domaine de la Garrique), Combe (Domaine de la Fourmone), Lambert Frères (Les Lambertins), and Mayre (Domaine du Mousquetaire).

The soil is siliceous and pebbly. The vineyards cover approximately 1,730 acres (700 hectares) of which about 370 acres (150 hectares) are in *Sarrians*, a neighboring village allowed to use the Côtes du Rhône Vacqueyras AC.

The predominant grape varieties in the red and rosé wines are Grenache, Mourvèdre, and Cinsault, which make up 60-70% of the vines. Syrah, as elsewhere in these parts, is increasing in importance. There are also small plantings of Carignan and Clairette. The harvest generally begins about September 20.

White Vacqueyras is the product of Clairette and Grenache blanc. This wine is best when very young as it tends to "madeirize" easily, particularly those whites made with a high percentage of Clairette grapes.

The rosé, like the white, is best in its youth.

Vacqueyras's best wine is its red, which is made in two styles, as in Châteauneuf-du-Pape—semi-carbonic maceration (see Chapter 17)—and the traditional method.

The semi-carbonic maceration wines are aged for about six months in cement or stainless steel before bottling. This wine should be drunk young. It retains its freshness and fruitiness for one to two years.

The traditional-style red wines are aged from one to two years in wood casks. They are best from about their fifth year and will live for a decade.

COTES DU RHONE VILLAGES (GARD)

The department of Gard, on the west bank of the Rhône, is known for its rosé wines, notably those of Tavel and Lirac. Not to be overlooked, though, are the rosés of *Chusclan*. While not generally as good as those of Tavel, they still can be a delight to drink. These pale, ruby-colored rosés were enjoyed by Louis XIV. Chusclan rosé has a fruity, somewhat aromatic, spicy perfume, which some say brings up the aroma of plums and acacia. It is full-bodied, dry, and fruity.

Up until 1971, AC Côtes du Rhône Chusclan was allowed only for rosé wines. Since then the reds have also been granted permission to use the village AC.

To qualify for the AC this rosé must attain its color from the skins. The juice is left in contact with the skins for six to ten hours, during which time the color "bleeds" from the skins, coloring the juice a rosy pink.

Vines are planted in stony soil on the right bank of the Rhône, opposite Orange and southwest of Pont-St.-Esprit. The vineyards extend across six villages on both banks of the Cèze river. The villages are, besides Chusclan, Bagnols-sur-Cèze, a small part of Codolet, Orsan, St.-Etienne-des-Sorts, and St.-Gervais.

Most of the wine of Chusclan is produced by the Cave Coopérative Les Vignerons de Chusclan. Gabriel Arnaud is a respected independent grower.

Every other year, since 1974, Chusclan has been the site of a festival for the wines of the Côtes du Rhône Villages. This fair alternates between Chusclan and the other villages.

Chusclan rosé is sometimes served locally mixed with a little Crème de Myrtilles (a blueberry liqueur) making an interesting variation on Kir.

The vineyards of *Laudun* are reputedly the oldest in the department of Gard. Julius Caesar is supposed to have camped nearby, and traces of vineyards from that time have been found.

Vines here are planted on the slopes and the flats, and spread out south from Laudun across the villages of Tresques and St.-Victor-la-Coste.

While red and rosé are also produced, Laudun is more noted for its delicate and fruity white wine.

Each of the three villages has its own co-op, but the best wine reputedly is a blend of the better wines from each commune. This wine is labeled Les 4 Chemins.

Other reputable producers of Laudun wines are Joseph Pelaquie, Edouard Pellaton, and Domaine Rousseau.

COTES DU RHONE VILLAGES WINES

Côtes du Rhône Villages red is generally a fast-maturing wine. It is full-flavored, fruity, and fresh. This wine is big enough to stand up to steaks, chops, and roasts.

The Villages white is best when young, within one to three years of the harvest. This wine goes well with veal and poultry, and with fish, particularly if prepared in a sauce.

The Côtes du Rhône Villages rosé is a good wine with ham or spicy hors d'oeuvres. It is at its best before its third, or in better vintages, fourth year. This fruity wine has a spicy aroma and a dry flavor. It is a full-bodied and assertive rosé.

THE COTES DU RHONE
FOR THE TRAVELER

ᑕᏕᏊᏱᎧ

19. THE CUISINE OF THE COTES DU RHONE

Geographically and gastronomically, the Côtes du Rhône extends into the regions of the Lyonnais, Dauphiné, Languedoc, and Provence.

LYONNAIS

The Lyonnais region includes the departments of Rhône and Loire. Here are the vineyards of Côte Rôtie, Condrieu, Château Grillet, and the northernmost section of St.-Joseph.

Lyon was dubbed the "capital of gastronomy" by the prince of gastronomes, Curnonsky. To the northeast is Bresse, the land of *poulardes de Bresse*—plump, succulent chickens; from the villages come excellent pork products, including the *saucissons de Lyon;* game from the Dombes; fresh fish from the Saône, the Loire, and the Rhône; sweet chestnuts from the mountains; and the famous Charolais beef. The Lyonnais is well known for its fruit, particularly the apricots of Ampuis. It is also noted for its vegetables, especially the onions of Roanne.

Lyon has been awarded more stars in the Michelin Guide Rouge for its cuisine than any other city except Paris. But this is not a cuisine of sophisticated sauces. Lyonnaise cooking, according to Waverley Root, is hearty and not subtle. *Pommes lyonnaises* are fried potatoes with onions, plenty of them. This vegetable has been such a favorite with the cooks of Lyon that to label a dish "Lyonnaise" is almost to say "with onions." The food is perhaps a bit heavy, but rich and delicious.

Some of the region's specialties to accompany your Côte Rôtie, St.-Joseph, Condrieu, and Château Grillet:

Omelette à la lyonnaise is seasoned with onions and parsley.

Quenelles financière are fish balls or dumplings garnished with giblets, sweetbreads, mushrooms, and truffles.

Quenelles de brochet, sauce Nantua—pike balls with a sauce of crayfish, butter, and cream.

Friture—fried whitebait. These small fish are crisply fried, whole, and popped into the mouth heads and all—delicious!

Matelote d'anguille is eel cooked in red wine with onions.

Matelote des poissons du Loire et Saône—a stew of fish from the Loire and Saône rivers.

Poulet aux écrevisses—chicken with crayfish.

Poularde demi-deuil—(chicken in "half-mourning") poached chicken, with slices of truffles tucked under the skin, served in a rich cream sauce and garnished with lamb sweetbreads.

Gâteau de foie blond de volailles—chicken-liver pie.

Gras-double à la lyonnaise—tripe cooked with onions and parsley.

Poularde en vessie—chicken sausage.

Veau en vessie—veal sausage.

Foie gras en crôute—liver pâté cooked in a pastry crust.

Tête de cochon roulée et pistachée—rolled pig's head with pistachio nuts.

Andouillette à la lyonnaise—tripe sausages cooked with onions and parsley.

Saucissons de Lyon—pork sausages flavored lightly with garlic.

Cervelas aux pistaches et aux truffes poché—poached pork sausages stuffed with pistachio nuts and truffles.

DAUPHINE

The Dauphiné stretches from the Alps to the Rhône river and includes the departments of Drôme and Isère. The wines of Hermitage, Crozes-Hermitage, and a few of the Côtes du Rhône Villages come from the western edge of the Dauphiné.

The cuisine of the Dauphiné is typically that of the mountains; it is robust and hearty with rib-sticking qualities. There isn't a lot of this influence in the area of the Dauphiné in the Rhône Valley, but you will see some of its specialties.

The Dauphiné is known for its spring vegetables; its fruit orchards, notably peaches and apricots; chestnuts; freshwater fish, particularly trout; baby quail; truffles; mushrooms, especially morels and cèpes; game; and mountain potatoes.

These potatoes usually accompany any dish served *à la dauphinoise*. These are thinly sliced and baked with milk, egg, a sprinkling of nutmeg, and topped with butter and grated Gruyère cheese browned to a crust. This style of potatoes is called *pommes de terre dauphinoises* or *gratin dauphinoise*.

Au gratin dishes—dishes prepared with a baked crust topping, usually of cheese—are common in the Dauphiné. Almost anything may be prepared *au gratin* here—not just potatoes, but macaroni, hashed meat, chard, cèpes, or even crayfish tails.

Some specialties of the Dauphiné that you might find

near the vineyard areas and enjoy with your Hermitage, Crozes-Hermitage, or Côtes du Rhône Villages wine:

Gratin de queues d'écrevisses—crayfish tails baked in a cream sauce under a crust of buttered bread crumbs.

Grives à la genièvre—thrush seasoned with juniper berries.

Pâté de grives—thrush pâté.

Salmis de grives—roasted thrush cut up and cooked in a wine sauce.

Cailleteau—baby quail.

Boeuf en daube—chunks of beef stewed in red wine seasoned with herbs and vegetables such as carrots, onions, and garlic.

Truffes marinées de Nyons—pickled truffles.

LANGUEDOC

The Languedoc includes the departments of Ardèche and Gard on the west bank of the Rhône where the wines of St.-Joseph, Cornas, St.-Péray, Lirac, Tavel, and the Villages wines of Chusclan and Gard are produced.

Waverley Root says of the Languedoc, in *The Food of France*, that "its raw materials are substantial and they are put together with gusto." This cuisine is peasant cooking, sure and simple. *A la languedocienne* generally describes a dish prepared with a garnish of tomatoes, eggplant, and cèpes, and often seasoned with garlic. Or such is their reputation; there are many exceptions to this rule. Cèpes are commonly found in the Languedoc, but the eggplant, tomato, and garlic are really more common in dishes served *à la provençale*. On the eastern edge of Languedoc, in the Rhône Valley, the influence of Provence is no doubt felt; they share many of the same gastronomic resources.

Some of the regional specialties to sample along with the wines of St.-Joseph, Cornas, St.-Péray, Lirac, Tavel, and Côtes du Rhône Villages:

Omelette de cèpes—mushroom omelette.

Truite à la meunière—river trout floured and sautéed in butter, sprinkled with parsley.

Truite au court-bouillon—river trout poached in aromatic broth.

Brandade de morue—salt cod mashed with garlic, milk, olive oil, and garnished with sliced truffles.

Morue à la languedocienne—salt cod, potatoes, and garlic mashed together into a paste.

Caneton aux olives—roast duckling with olives.

Râble de lièvre à la crème—saddle of hare in cream sauce.

PROVENCE

Provence, the land of sun and shimmering blue skies, is also a land of bright cuisine—piquant and colorful.

The department of Vaucluse in the southern Côtes du Rhône is in the region of Provence. From here we have the wines of Châteauneuf-du-Pape, Gigondas, Rasteau, Beaumes de Venise, and the Côtes du Rhône Villages of Vaucluse.

Dishes described *à la provençale* will almost certainly be accompanied by cooked tomatoes and flavored with garlic. Tomatoes are used in practically everything done in the style of Provence, and the garlic, often seen hanging along windows and doorways, has been called "the Provençal truffle."

But perhaps the most important ingredient of all in Provençal cooking is the olive. Olive trees are a common sight, growing in the vineyards as well as in olive groves. Olive oil is used in cooking the majority of Provençal dishes. And when the dish is not cooked, olive oil is the major ingredient used in the dressing put on the raw food.

Aromatic herbs such as lavender and thyme grow wild in the Côtes du Rhône area of Provence. Savory, sage, rosemary, and basil also enter frequently into the cuisine of this region as *herbes de Provence* and *aromates.*

With the wines of the region—Châteauneuf-du-Pape, Gigondas, Rasteau, Beaumes de Venise, and the Côtes du Rhône Villages—the specialties of the region:

Tapenade, also called *caviar provençale*—black olives, finely chopped or crushed into a paste, liberally seasoned with garlic, aromatic herbs, and perhaps anchovy, mixed all together with olive oil.

Soupe à l'ail—garlic soup floating pieces of toast under a crust of cheese.

Aïgo bouïdo à la ménagère—another garlic soup, this one floating a poached egg.

Pistou—vegetable soup flavored with garlic and aromatic basil.

Aïoli—mayonnaise generously flavored with crushed garlic; served on vegetables, egg dishes, and fish. It goes very well on shrimp and crayfish.

Ratatouille—hot or cold mixture of chopped tomatoes, eggplant, and zucchini, perhaps onions, stewed together with garlic in olive oil.

Cèpes à la provençale—cèpe mushrooms in olive oil with onions and garlic.

Asperge vauclusienne—no, it's not asparagus—would you believe artichokes, stuffed with chopped ham and seasoned with herbs.

Loup au fenouil—sea bass cooked with fennel.

Rouget au romarin—red mullet flavored with rosemary.

Grenouilles sauté provençale—frogs' legs breaded and sautéed in olive oil and butter, and seasoned with garlic and parsley.

Carré de porc rôti à la provençale—roast pork which has been stuck with sage leaves and marinated in thyme, laurel (bay), garlic, and olive oil.

Agneau au lait—suckling lamb.

Daube de boeuf à la provençale—cubes of beef browned in olive oil and stewed in white wine with seasonings and herbs and bacon, tomatoes, carrots, onions, garlic, mushrooms, black olives, and a little orange peel.

Marcassin—young wild boar.

Fromage blanc au crème fraîche—fresh mild goat cheese topped with thick fresh cream.

Pasteque melon—similar to our honeydew melon. This is just the thing with the *vin doux naturel*.

You'll find watermelons (unusual in Europe), *patate* (sweet potatoes), peaches, apricots, quince, cherries, and almonds, among Provence's bounty.

CHEESES OF THE COTES DU RHONE AND VICINITY

Banon is produced on small farms in the departments of Drôme, Isère, and Vaucluse from goats' or sheep's milk. The goats'-milk Banon can be found from late spring to early autumn; the sheep's-milk variety is available in spring and summer. A cows'-milk version made in commercial dairies is available all year round. This soft, natural-rind cheese is made in small discs (3 inches in diameter, 1 inch thick) weighing about 4 ounces each. Banon is wrapped in chestnut leaves. Its texture is firm, yet yielding to the touch. It has a mild, slightly milky flavor. Banon is a good cheese to eat with St.-Joseph, red and white; Condrieu; Lirac, rosé and white; Gigondas rosé; Côtes du Rhône (Villages), red, white and rosé.

Banon au Pebre d'Ai (see *Poivre d'Ane*).

Bleu du Pelvoux is a soft, blue cheese with an internal mold. It is made in the Dauphiné from cows' milk.

Bleu de Queyras is similar to Bleu du Pelvoux.

Bleu de Sassenage, related to Bleu du Pelvoux and Bleu de Queyras, is made in dairies in the Isère Valley. This soft, blue cheese has a natural rind. It comes in large discs (12 inches in diameter, 3 inches thick) weighing approximately 12 pounds. Sometimes goats' milk is added to the cows' milk. It is available year-round. All of these cows'-milk blue cheeses go well with the red wines of Châteauneuf-du-Pape, Gigondas, Cornas, Hermitage, and Côtes du Rhône (Villages).

Cachat, also known as *Tomme du Mont Ventoux*, is a fresh, salted sheep's-milk cheese. This soft, white cheese is sweet and creamy with a slight milky flavor. It is made on farms during the summer and eaten while it is fresh. This a good cheese with Gigondas rosé and Côtes du Rhône (Villages) rosé or white. Cachat is similar to the Provençal Brousses.

Picodon de St.-Agreve is similar to Picodon de Valréas. This soft cheese from Languedoc comes in small discs (3 inches by 1 inch) of about 4½ ounces. The rind may be a light bluish or light golden color. It has a firm texture and a slightly nutty flavor. This cheese would go well with Côtes du Rhône (Villages) red, white, or rosé; or with the rosés of Lirac, Tavel, or Gigondas.

Picodon de Dieulefit is a small, irregular, disc-shaped cheese (2½-3 inches in diameter, 1 inch thick) with a soft, natural, golden-reddish rind weighing 3 to 3½ ounces. It is made from goats' milk on farms in the Dauphiné near Montélimar. Its texture is firm but not hard. It is moderately sharp in flavor. The season for this cheese is the end of the summer and in the autumn.

Picodon de Valréas is a soft, semi-fresh goat cheese from the Comtat Venaissin. It is made in small discs (diameter—3 inches, thickness—1 inch) weighing about 4 ounces. Picodon de Valréas has a thin natural rind. It is supple and yielding to the touch, and has a slightly nutty flavor. Look for Picodon from the end of the spring through the beginning of the fall. This is a good cheese to go with Côtes du Rhône (Villages) red, white, or rosé; Lirac rosé and white; Gigondas rosé; Châteauneuf-du-Pape white.

Poivre d'Ane (Pebre d'Ai) is produced in the Comtat Venaissin, Dauphiné, and Provence. Dairies produce a cows'-milk version; farms, the sheep's- or goats'-milk varieties. This cheese is made in small discs (3 inches in diameter, 1 inch thick) weighing about 4 ounces. It has a natural rind that is covered with sprigs of savory. The color beneath this covering ranges from bluish- to yellowish-white. This mild, aromatic cheese goes well with the fruity white, rosé, and red wines of the Côtes du Rhône (Villages); Tavel rosé; Lirac rosé and white; Gigondas rosé; St.-Joseph red and white.

Rigotte de Condrieu is a cows'-milk cheese made in small dairies year-round in the northern Côtes du Rhône. The soft natural rind is tinted red with annatto. This small cylinder-shaped cheese is about 1½ inches high and across, and weighs about 2 ounces. Its texture is firm, yet yielding to the touch. Rigotte is mild-flavored, with a somewhat milky taste. It goes well with St.-Péray (still) wines, St.-Joseph white, Crozes-Hermitage white, Condrieu, or Côtes du Rhône (Villages) white.

Saint-Marcellin, at one time made on farms from goats' milk, is produced today from cows' milk in dairies in the Isère Valley year-round. This small, disc-shaped cheese (3 inches by 1 inch) weighing 3 ounces has a light bluish-gray rind and a supple texture. It is mild in flavor with a somewhat milky flavor. The white wines of St.-Joseph, Condrieu, St.-Péray (still), Crozes-Hermitage, and Côtes du Rhône Villages should go well with this cheese, as should the Côtes du Rhône Villages rosés.

Tomme usually refers to a semi-hard or semi-soft, mild-flavored cheese produced in the mountains. At one time *tommes* were the product of goats' milk or sheep's milk, but today cows' milk is sometimes used. Oftentimes the village name will be appended to the word *tomme*. *Tomme* cheeses would go well with the white wines of Lirac, St.-Joseph, St.-Péray, Crozes-Hermitage, Condrieu, Côtes du Rhône Villages; the rosés of Lirac, Tavel, Gigondas, Côtes du Rhône (Villages); and the reds of St.-Joseph, Crozes-Hermitage, and Côtes du Rhône Villages.

Tomme de Camargue is a sheep's-milk *tomme*, flavored with thyme or bayleaf. This small, square-shaped (2½ inch by 2½ inch by ½ inch) cheese is produced around Arles. It is soft, mild, and creamy with the flavor and aroma of the herb used in its making. This *tomme* is a better choice with the white wines than the reds.

Tomme de Combovin is a goats'-milk cheese from Drôme. It has a soft, natural, pale bluish rind sometimes with red speckles. Combovin is round (4 inches in diameter, 1 inch thick) and weighs about 8 ounces, perhaps a bit more. It is mild in flavor and slightly nutty. This cheese is a better choice with rosés than whites.

Tomme de Corps, produced in Drôme, is made in a

cylinder shape (about 3 inches high and 4 inches across) weighing nearly a pound. This is a goats' milk *tomme*. It has a bluish-gray rind, is firm to the touch, and has a somewhat nutty flavor. This cheese goes well with the whites and rosés of the Côtes du Rhône.

Tomme de Crest, another goats'-milk *tomme*, is from the Dauphiné. Tomme de Crest comes in small round discs (2½ inches in diameter, 1 inch thick) weighing 3½ ounces. It has a bluish rind. It is firm yet yielding in texture, and has a nutty flavor. This is a cheese for the whites and rosés of the Côtes du Rhône.

Tomme de Romans is a cows'-milk *tomme* from the Dauphiné. It is made in discs (4½ inches in diameter, 1 inch thick) weighing 9 ounces. This cheese has a bluish-gray rind and it is yielding to the touch. In flavor it is mildly nutty, yet slightly sour. It is a good accompaniment to the red wines of the Côtes du Rhône, including the Villages reds and those of Lirac, St.-Joseph, Crozes-Hermitage, and Cornas.

RECOMMENDED FOOD-WINE COMBINATIONS

APERITIF
St.-Péray *mousseux*, brut
Cairanne *vin doux naturel*
Rasteau *vin doux naturel*
Tavel rosé

HORS D'OEUVRES
FISH
Côtes du Rhône (Villages) white
Lirac white
Tavel rosé

MEAT
Côtes du Rhône (Villages) rosé
Lirac rosé
Gigondas rosé
Tavel rosé

FISH
FRESHWATER—GRILLED, PAN-FRIED, POACHED
Château Grillet
Condrieu
Lirac white
Crozes-Hermitage white
St.-Joseph white
St.-Péray, still

FRESHWATER—IN SAUCES
Crozes-Hermitage white
St.-Péray, still
St.-Joseph white

SALTWATER—BAKED, POACHED, PAN-FRIED
Châteauneuf-du-Pape white
Côtes du Rhône (Villages) white
Lirac white
Hermitage white

SALTWATER—IN SAUCES
Côtes du Rhône (Villages) white
Côtes du Rhône (Villages) rosé
Châteauneuf-du-Pape white
Gigondas rosé
Lirac white

Lirac rosé
Tavel rosé
Hermitage white

SHELLFISH
Château Grillet
Condrieu
Châteauneuf-du-Pape white
Tavel rosé

FISH IN CASSEROLE
Côtes du Rhône (Villages) white
St.-Péray, still

FISH CHOWDER, BOUILLABAISSE
Côtes du Rhône (Villages) white
Côtes du Rhône (Villages) rosé

COLD CUTS, CHARCUTERIE
Lirac white
Lirac rosé
Côtes du Rhône (Villages) rosé
Côtes du Rhône (Villages) white
Hermitage white
Crozes-Hermitage white

POULTRY
CHICKEN
Château Grillet
Côtes du Rhône (Villages) white
Côtes du Rhône (Villages) rosé
Lirac white

St.-Péray white
Lirac rosé
Tavel rosé

TURKEY
Châteauneuf-du-Pape white
Côtes du Rhône Villages white
Côtes du Rhône Villages rosé
Hermitage white
Ravel rosé
Gigondas rosé

DUCK
Châteauneuf-du-Pape red
St.-Joseph red
Lirac red

POULTRY IN CASSEROLE
Côtes du Rhône Villages white
Côtes du Rhône Villages rosé
Lirac white
Crozes-Hermitage white
St.-Péray white
Gigondas rosé

VEAL
Château Grillet
Châteauneuf-du-Pape white
Lirac white
Hermitage white
St.-Joseph white
St.-Joseph red
Côtes du Rhône Villages red

PORK
Château Grillet
Châteauneuf-du-Pape white
Hermitage white
St.-Joseph white
Côtes du Rhône Villages rosé
Gigondas rosé
Tavel rosé
Crozes-Hermitage red

HAM
Côtes du Rhône (Villages) rosé
Gigondas rosé
Lirac rosé
Tavel rosé
St.-Joseph red

LAMB
Crozes-Hermitage red
Côtes du Rhône Villages red
Lirac red

BEEF—ROASTS, STEAKS; GRILLED, BROILED
Châteauneuf-du-Pape red
Cornas
Côtes du Rhône Villages red
Crozes-Hermitage red
Côte Rôtie
Gigondas red
Hermitage red
Lirac red

GAME
Châteauneuf-du-Pape red
Hermitage red
Côte Rôtie
Cornas
Gigondas red

CHEESE
MILD
Château Grillet
Condrieu
Tavel rosé
St.-Joseph white
Crozes-Hermitage white
STRONG
Gigondas red
Châteauneuf-du-Pape red
Hermitage red
Lirac red

GOAT
Côtes du Rhône Villages white
Lirac white

FRUIT
Cairanne *vin doux naturel*
Beaumes de Venise *vin doux naturel*
Rasteau *vin doux naturel* white
St.-Péray *mousseux, demi-sec*

NUTS
Cairanne *vin doux naturel*
Rasteau *vin doux naturel*

20. HISTORICAL SIGHTS IN THE COTES DU RHONE

The Côtes du Rhône is a fascinating region to visit not only for its vineyards and its wines, and regional cuisine, but also for its scenic beauty and its historical sights.

Using Avignon as a base, you could travel south to St.-Rémy-de-Provence and Les Baux-de-Provence, then southwest to Arles. Heading northwest you arrive at Nîmes. From there, going northwest to the Pont du Gard and then east brings you back to Avignon. This area boasts some of the most magnificent Roman theaters, triumphal arches, aqueducts, and ruins of Roman cities in Europe.

If you'd prefer taking in the historical sights along with the vineyard areas in the southern Côtes du Rhône, you might head northeast from Avignon to Carpentras. From there, north to the wine towns of Beaumes de Venise, Vacqueyras, Gigondas, Sablet, and Séguret. Continuing north, you arrive at Vaison-la-Romaine. From Vaison, traveling southwest through the wine towns of Roaix, Rasteau, and Cairanne, you arrive at Orange. Going south you pass through Châteauneuf-du-Pape and Roquemaure. From there a slight detour west will take you to Lirac and Tavel. Continuing southeast, you come to Villeneuve-les-Avignon and then back to Avignon.

The northern Côtes du Rhône, from Vienne to Valence, will take you through the wine regions of Côte Rôtie, Condrieu, Château Grillet, St.-Joseph, Hermitage, Crozes-

Hermitage, Cornas, and St.-Péray. The Roman ruins at Vienne are the most impressive in the northern region.

Arles is a treasure trove of Roman relics. The Roman theater, begun during the time of Emperor Augustus, took 150 years to complete. During July this theater is the scene of a drama festival.

To visit the underground galleries of the Roman forum, you must enter through the Museum of Christian Art.

The 25,000-seat Roman arena is used every Sunday during the summer months for the Course à la Cocarde, a Provençal bullfight where the bull, not the man, is the hero. (During June real bullfights, where the bull is killed, are held on weekends.)

Les Alyscamps was a pagan burial ground, and was transformed during the Middle Ages into a Christian cemetery.

Frederick Barbarossa was crowned king of Arles in 1178 in the Romanesque Church of St.-Trophime, which dates back to Carolingian times. The twelfth-century cloisters behind the church boast some fine Romanesque statuary.

On the Place de la République, the main square of Arles, are a Roman obelisk and a seventeeth-century town hall, now used as the Museum of Pagan Art.

The Arlaten Museum offers a view of provençal life. The Baths of Constantine are the best preserved in Provence.

In August a folklore fête is held on the Trinquetaille bridge.

Avignon is still surrounded by its battlements, towers, and gates, which extend for three miles to encircle the old town.

The Palais des Papes is an imposing structure built during the reign of the popes at Avignon. The inner courtyard of the popes' palace is the site of a drama festival during the summer.

The Petit Palais was the episcopal palace of the fourteenth and fifteenth centuries.

The twelfth-century Romanesque cathedral of Notre Dame, restored in the fifteenth and seventeenth centuries, houses the tombs of popes John XXII (1316-1334) and Benedict XII (1334-1342), the former a masterpiece of fourteenth-century Gothic art.

The park, Rocher des Doms, offers a magnificent panoramic view of the environs.

The Musée Calvet, housed in a beautiful eighteenth-century building, contains a splendid art collection, antique furniture, early paintings from the Avignon school, and Greek and Roman art.

The grave of John Stuart Mill, author of *On Liberty*, is in the old cemetery.

The Lapidary Museum has an important collection of Gallo-Roman, medieval, and Renaissance sculptures.

And for all of you who remember the song ("Sur le pont d'Avignon, l'on y danse, l'on y danse; Sur le pont d'Avignon, l'on y danse tout en rond.") one sight which definitely cannot be missed is Pont St.-Bénézet, whether to dance on or merely to observe as a site of history and legend. As the story goes, Bénézet, a peasant lad, heard heavenly voices telling him to build a bridge across the Rhône. This being a rather overwhelming task for the young boy, he went to town to enlist some aid. When he approached the town officials with his story, they dismissed him as a fool, as did the religious authorities. So he set to work on his mission unaided, alone. Some of the townsfolk became convinced of his story when he laid the foundation stone. He chose a huge boulder a short distance off, shouldered it with the greatest of ease, and sauntered on down to the Rhône, where he plopped it down at the river's edge. At that, some of the men of the town became believers and pitched in to help him out. With this help (but apparently no more divine assistance) the bridge was built in the span of eleven years.

The bridge, nearly 3,000 feet across, linked the Territories of the Empire with the Territories of the Kingdom. Of twenty-two original arches, only four now remain. On the bridge is a little chapel to Saint Nicholas embodying both Romanesque and Gothic styles.

In *Carpentras*, the former capital of the Comtat Venaissin, there are a number of interesting historical sights. The Roman triumphal arch from the first century is carved with an unusual bas-relief.

The hulking fourteenth-century Port d'Orange is all that is now left of the medieval ramparts. Building on the fifteenth-century Cathedral of Saint Siffrein, with its flamboyant Gothic portal, was begun by the antipope Benedict XIII.

The seventeenth-century archbishops' palace, now the Palace of Justice, and the eighteenth-century Hôtel Dieu are also of interest.

The synagogue, built in the fifteenth century (and reconstructed in the seventeenth and eighteenth), is the oldest synagogue in France.

Châteauneuf-du-Pape is dominated by the ruins of the old papal summer palace at the crest of the hill rising above the village.

In *Gigondas*, still surrounded by its medieval walls, is the fifth-century chapel of Saint Cosme.

Les Baux-de-Provence is a medieval ghost town below the ruins of a once proud castle perched on jagged gray rock. Restored Renaissance houses, a thirteenth-century fortress tower, and medieval churches crowd into this picturesque setting. Some of the churches were built into the hollowed-out rock of the cliff itself.

Close by is the eerie Valley of the Inferno said to have inspired Dante.

The nearby bauxite (which takes its name from Baux) quarries are strangely cut into the soft white stone, presenting the impression of Aztec buildings and temples.

In September, the Festival of the Olive Tree is celebrated here.

Nîmes (the Roman city of Nemausus) is the site of the best-preserved Roman amphitheater in the world. During July and August music and drama festivals are held in this impressive setting.

From the vantage point of the first-century Roman tower, Tour Magne, you can see the Mediterranean on a clear day.

The eleventh-century cathedral of Notre Dame et St.-Castor has an ancient third-century chapel.

The Maison Carrée, the "square house," is a remarkably well preserved Roman temple from the first century.

A vast Roman arena, the ruins of the Temple of Diana, and a Museum of Antiquities containing Gallo-Roman art including the Venus of Nîmes remind one of the days when Provence was under Roman rule.

A festival of the vine is held here during October.

The city of *Orange* boasts a 10,000-seat Roman amphitheater from 35 BC, the site of music and drama festivals in July and August, and where sound and light performances are also staged.

Remains of several temples, a Roman gymnasium, and the Arc de Triomphe of Tiberius from 49 BC give some indication of the Roman influence once felt here.

The *Pont du Gard* is a magnificent Roman aqueduct

built between green wooded hills. The three tiers of stone arches span the Gard, or Gardon, river.

The ruins of the Gallo-Roman city of Glanum, destroyed in the barbarian invasions, as well as the remains of a second-century BC Gallo-Greek city unearthed in recent excavations make *St.-Rémy-de-Provence* one of the more interesting places to visit.

Across the street from Glanum are Les Antiques, a Roman arch and the small Mausoleum of the Princes of Youth, grandsons of Emperor Augustus.

A museum of Provençal folklore and the Romanesque cloisters of St.-Paul-de-Mansolé add an extra dimension to the interesting sights here.

The medieval hillside town of *Vaison-la-Romaine* is at the foot of a twelfth-century fortified château of the Counts of Toulouse. It has a sixth- to seventh-century Romanesque cathedral with cloisters dating from the eleventh to twelfth centuries. In the Chapel of Saint Guenin is a unique triangular Romanesque apse.

Below the medieval town is a Gallo-Roman town from the second century BC. Here are the remains of houses, baths, paved streets, mosaic floors, and one of the best preserved Roman theaters in the area. In July this theater is the site of a series of artistic events.

Vienne is the site of the Temple of Augustus and Livia, preserved in near-mint condition, and a Roman theater built into the hillside.

Other interesting sights: the Pyramide monument, the twelfth-century Romanesque cloisters, the cathedral of Saint Maurice dating from the twelfth century and decorated with a remarkable array of high reliefs, the lapidary museum in the Church of Saint Pierre, and the sixth-century Abbey of Saint André-le-Bas.

Across the river, at St.-Romain-en-Gal, are the ruins of a Gallo-Roman city.

Villeneuve-les-Avignon, across the river from Avignon at the other end of Pont Saint Bénézet, is the site of the twelfth-century tower of Philippe le Bel.

Fort Saint-André was built there in the fourteenth century. There is also a Carthusian monastery, Chartreuse du Val de Bénédiction.

APPENDIX A

ELEMENTS OF PRODUCTION FOR THE APPELLATIONS OF THE COTES DU RHONE

Appellation	Chaptalization Allowed	Minimum Alcohol	Maximum gals/acre	Yield hl/ha
Beaumes de Venise [1]	no	15% [7]	300	28
Châteauneuf-du-Pape [2,3]	no	12.5%	375	35
Château Grillet [3]	no	11%	343	32
Condrieu [3]	yes	11%	321	30
Cornas [2]	no	10.5%	375	35
Côte Rôtie [2]	yes	10%	375	35
Côtes du Rhône [2,3,4]	no	11%	535	50
Côtes du Rhône Villages [3,4]	no	12%	375	35
Côtes du Rhône Villages [2]	no	12.5%	375	35
Crozes-Hermitage [2,3]	yes	10%	428	40
Gigondas [2,4]	no	12.5%	375	35
Hermitage [2,3]	yes	10%	428	40
Hermitage vins de paille	no	14%	300	28

Appellation	Chaptalization Allowed	Minimum Alcohol	Maximum gals/acre	Yield hl/ha
Lirac [2,3,4]	no	11.5%	375	35
Rasteau [1,6]	no	15% [7]	321	30
St.-Joseph [2,3]	no	10%	428	40
St.-Péray [3,5]	no	10%	428	40
Tavel [4]	no	11%	450	42

1. VDN (vin doux naturel)
2. Red
3. White
4. Rosé
5. Mousseux (sparkling)
6. VDL (vin de liqueur)

7. Total Richness (actual alcohol plus potential alcohol, i.e., sugar) must be at least 21.5%. The minimum listed above refers to the actual alcohol alone.

APPENDIX B

EXTENT OF VINEYARDS BY APPELLATIONS AND

	VAUCLUSE		GARD		DROME	
	ACRES	HECTARES	ACRES	HECTARES	ACRES	HECTARES
Côtes du Rhône (including CdR Villages)	43,960	17,790	16,408	6,640	22,123	8,953
Beaumes de Venise VDN	457	185				
Château Grillet						
Châteauneuf-du-Pape	7,611	3,080				
Condrieu						
Cornas						
Côte Rôtie						
Crozes-Hermitage					1,359	550
Gigondas	2,446	990				
Hermitage					304	123
Lirac			1,722	697		
St.-Joseph						
St.-Péray						
Tavel			1,779	720		
TOTAL *	54,474	22,045	19,909	8,057	23,786	9,626

* Totals have been rounded off to whole numbers.

DEPARTMENT WITHIN THE COTES DU RHONE (1973)

ARDECHE		RHONE		LOIRE		TOTAL	
ACRES	HECTARES	ACRES	HECTARES	ACRES	HECTARES	ACRES	HECTARES
470	190	5.44	2.20	9.88	4.00	82,976	33,579
						457	185
				4.21	2.11	4.21	2.11
						7,611	3,080
0.67	0.27	14.83	6.00	14.83	6.00	30	12.27
185	75					185	75
		178	72			178	72
						1,359	550
						2,466	990
						304	123
						1,722	697
284	115			17.30	7.00	301	122
138	56					138	56
						1,779	720
1079	436	198	80	47	19	99,494	40,264

BIBLIOGRAPHY

Bailly, Robert. *Histoire du Vin de Vaucluse.*

Churchill, Creighton. *The Great Wine Rivers.* New York: Macmillan, 1971.

Dorozynski, Alexander and Bell, Bibiane. *The Wine Book.* New York: Western Publishing (Golden Press), 1969.

Galet, P. *Cépages et Vignobles de France,* Vols. II and III. Montpellier, France: Vol II-1957, Vol III-1962.

Gold, Alex, ed. *Wines and Spirits of the World.* Chicago: Follett, 1972.

Hallgarten, Peter. *Côtes du Rhône* (pamphlet). London: Wineographs, 1965.

Healy, Maurice. *Stay Me with Flagons.* London: Michael Joseph, 1940.

Huguier, Philippe. *Vins des Côtes du Rhône.* Marseille: 1974.

Hyams, Edward. *Dionysus-A Social History of Wine.* New York: Macmillan, 1965.

Jacquelin, Louis and Poulain, René. *The Wines and Vineyards of France.* New York: G.P. Putnam's Sons, 1962.

Jobe, Joseph, ed. *Great Book of Wine.* New York: Crown, 1974.

Johnson, Hugh. *World Atlas of Wine.* New York: Simon & Schuster, 1972.

Lichine, Alexis. *Encyclopedia of Wines and Spirits.* New York: Knopf, 1967.

———. *Wines of France.* New York: Knopf, 1969.

Ordish, George. *The Great Wine Blight.* New York: Charles Scribner's Sons, 1972.

Price, Pamela Vandyke. *The Taste of Wine*. New York: Random House, 1975.

Root, Waverley. *The Food of France*. New York: Knopf, 1958.

Saintsbury, George. *Notes on a Cellar Book*. New York: Macmillan, 1933.

Schoonmaker, Frank. *Encyclopedia of Wine*. New York: Hastings House, 1973.

Simon, André. *The Noble Grapes and the Great Wines of France*. New York: McGraw-Hill, 1957.

Wildman, Frederick S., Jr. *A Wine Tour of France*. New York: Morrow, 1972.

Younger, William. *Gods, Men and Wine*. New York: Humanities Press, 1966.

INDEX

Allègre, Abbot, quoted, 120
Abeille, Jean, 159, 168
Aging, 116; at Cairanne, 178; at Château Grillet, 71; at Châteauneuf, 164; at Condrieu, 65-66; at Cornas, 81; at Crozes-Hermitage, 106; at Côte Rôtie, 58-59; at Gigondas, 140; at Hermitage, 89, 99; at Lirac, 126-27; at Rasteau, 115; at Tavel, 134; at Vacqueyras, 179-80
Aigle, village of, 22
Aix-en-Provence, 27
Alary et Fils, 177
Albigenses, 144
Alcohol content: brandy and marc, 42-43; wines, 42, 208-09
Allobrogica grape, 26
Altesse grape. *See* Roussette
Amadieu, Pierre, 141
American rootstock, imported, 32; and phylloxera, 32
Amido, Christian, 135
Amigne, 21
Ampelographers, 28
Ampuis, town of, 51
Appellation Controlée (AC): enforcing agency of, 33-34; by Department, 34-35; local, 36; meaning of, 33; regional, 35-36, 80

Appellation d'origine, 43
Appellation reglementée, 43
Appellations by type, 37
Archimbaud, 179; Jean et Maurice, 141
Ardèche, department of, wine production, 34, 211
Ardèche, river, 23
Ardoix, town of, 77
Arène, Luc, 176
Arles, historical sights of, 202
Armenier, Elie, 159
Arnaud, Gabriel, 180
Arnaud, Louis, 159
Arras-sur-Rhone, town of, 77
Arvine, 21
Assemat, J., 127
Audance, town of, 77
Avignon, historical sights of, 202-04
Avril, Paul, 159
Ay, François, 141
Aygues, river, 23, 112

Bagnols-sur-Cèze, village of, 180
Ban de Vendange, 126
Banon (cheese), 191
Bardelli, 178
Barge, Pierre, 58, 60
Barges, 45
Barjac, Guy de, 82
Barrel making. *See* coopering

215